Sales Management Role Plays

Sales Management Role Plays

WILLIAM C. MONCRIEF
Texas Christian University

SHANNON H. SHIPP
Texas Christian University

HarperCollins*CollegePublishers*

Executive Editor: Anne Elizabeth Smith
Development Editor: John F. O'Callaghan
Project Coordination and Text Design: Ruttle, Shaw & Wetherill, Inc.
Cover Design: Kay Petronio
Production Manager/Administrator/Assistant: Hilda Koparanian
Compositor: BookMasters, Inc.
Printer and Binder: Malloy Lithography, Inc.
Cover Printer: Malloy Lithography, Inc.

Sales Management Role Plays

Library of Congress Cataloging-in-Publication Data

Moncrief, William C.
Sales management role plays / William C. Moncrief, Shannon H. Shipp.
p. cm.
ISBN 0-673-46904-2
1. Sales management. I. Shipp, Shannon. II. Title.
HF5438.4.M66 1993
568.8'1—dc20 93–26370
CIP

94 95 96 9 8 7 6 5 4 3 2

This book is dedicated to our parents and in-laws
Bill and Mary Claire Moncrief
James and Martha Shipp
Roy and Jeanne Greenlee
John and Betty Zeb Williams

CONTENTS

PREFACE

Sales Management Role Plays was written to make the material covered in the sales management class more exciting and immediate to students. The overriding purpose of the book is to give students a chance to learn about important sales management topics such as motivation, leadership, compensation, training, selection, and ethics by participating in real sales management situations in which those skills are developed and practiced.

Role plays are widely used in sales training. One survey shows that videotaping of sales encounters is used by as many as 89 percent of the Fortune 500 companies in the training of their salespeople. Role plays are also widely used in personal selling classes to introduce students to the nuances of the sales encounter. Despite their popularity in sales training and in the personal selling class, no role play text has heretofore been developed for sales *management* courses. *Sales Management Role Plays* is designed specifically to introduce students to situations they will likely encounter as sales *managers*.

Sales Management Role Plays begins in Part I with an introduction to role playing. The text also provides hints to students for approaching the role play assignment and for videotaping the role play. Of course, the role plays can also be performed live in class. The role plays are based on sales management situations that occur at a large pharmaceutical company named Pharmiceaux. The Pharmiceaux case is found in Part II of the text. While the company and the situations are fictional, they are based on the experiences of hundreds of salespeople. Each role play has been scrutinized by sales professionals for accuracy and realism.

Part III of the text contains the role plays: one per chapter. Each chapter begins with a brief discussion of the topic of the role play (e.g., compensation). The introduction to the topic of the role play is followed by the role play itself. The role play consists of a series of scenarios for students to act out live or on videotape. The scenarios are followed by a description of the characters that appear in the role play. The descriptions of the characters include not only the names and job titles, but also information about the person's hobbies and interests. There is also "grapevine" information about each character, which can range from the individual's likelihood for career advancement to his or her relationships with subordinates or superiors. Each character has a male and a female version to allow for maximum flexibility in assigning students to teams and the characters reflect the ethnic diversity in today's sales organizations.

This text is designed to be used as an adjunct to any of the leading sales management texts on the market. The role plays are modular. No role play depends on a previous role play, or acts as background for an upcoming role play. As a result, the role plays can be assigned in any order. This allows professors to tailor the role play presentations to the order of the material presented in their course.

Over the past ten years, the role plays in the book have been developed and classroom-tested by the authors. The role plays have been used and critiqued by hundreds of students and salespeople. In preparation for publication, the role plays were tested by professors at several state and private universities in graduate and undergraduate sales management classes. Without exception, the students in the classes reported that the role plays were a valuable adjunct to the texts they used in the class. In addition, professors reported that the resulting class discussions were livelier, more wide-ranging, and more stimulating than when role plays were not used.

Sales Management Role Plays also comes with a comprehensive *Instructor's Manual* and VHS videotape. The *Instructor's Manual* contains the following:

- Thorough discussion of each role play.
- Different solutions to each role play—with a complete discussion of the strengths and weaknesses of each solution.
- A guide to the use of role plays for instructors who have never used this method of instruction.
- A set of handouts for students that deal with taping role plays.
- A sample syllabus integrating role plays with a standard set of topics covered in the sales management course.
- A grid showing how the role plays correspond to the order of topics for several leading sales management texts.

Adopters also receive upon adoption through their local representative a VHS videotape of student presentations of each role play, along with complete scripts and authors' comments. These can be used to prepare for the class in which a given role play will be shown, or to substitute for role plays for which a student team was not assigned.

Numerous people have made this text possible. Our thanks for the support we have received go to our Dean, Kirk Downey, and from our colleagues in the Marketing Department at TCU. Our graduate assistants, Luis Andrade, Sarah Tempel, and Byron Simpson have spent many hours proofing, developing characters, and gathering research for the Pharmiceaux case. Thanks also to Jinger Lord who spent many hours transcribing the videotapes and preparing the *Instructor's Manual*. Our thanks also to Fran Eller for her tireless and cheerful approach to typing all the drafts of the manuscript.

Several reviewers helped make the final version of the text much stronger. Professor Ramon Avila, Ball State University; Professor Joseph Bellizzi, Arizona State University; Professor Robert Erffmeyer, University of Wisconsin, Eau Claire; Professor Mark Johnston, Rollins College; Professor Raymond LaForge, University of Louisville; and Professor Bradley O'Hara, Southeastern Louisiana University thoroughly reviewed the text and made numerous suggestions for improvement. The responsibility for any remaining errors, of course, is ours.

We owe a major debt to Scott Wilson, who prepared the videotapes that accompany the *Instructor's Manual*. With a limited budget, incredibly short deadlines, and student actors, Scott was able to accomplish miracles.

A great deal of credit for the form of the text goes to our publisher, HarperCollins. Thanks to our editor, Anne Smith, and her editorial assistant, Jay O'Callaghan, who motivated us and worked very hard to ensure the highest quality text obtainable. A special thanks to Susan Katz, our publisher, who has been very supportive throughout the project.

While it would not be possible to list all of the students who have used or critiqued the role plays over the years, much of the credit for the role plays in this text goes to them. They challenged us to improve role plays that were unrealistic or impossible to resolve, and the fruit of their comments is contained in this text.

Last, thanks to our families. They are the ones who have had to work around our writing deadlines, and without their continued love and support, this book would not have been possible.

PART I
INTRODUCTION

INTRODUCTION

The purpose of *Sales Management Role Plays* is to provide you, the student, with a practical approach to exploring concepts in sales management. This book uses role plays to introduce and reinforce sales management concepts. Role plays consist of two or more "characters" interacting to present, discuss, and solve a given problem in sales management.

The concept of role playing certainly is not new. Industry has been using role plays for decades to help train personnel. If you join a professional sales organization, the odds are high that you will perform role plays during the interview process and certainly as a part of your training. For many of you, role playing will be an important component of training throughout your career. Through role plays, salespeople learn to handle customer objections, to recognize different types of customers, and to become more sensitive to body language and other nuances of the sales encounter. Professional sales organizations use role plays because they provide a valuable opportunity for new salespeople to practice their sales presentation skills and have their presentations critiqued by others before they use those skills with an actual customer. Role plays are also an important tool for experienced salespeople to become familiar with selling a new product or dealing with a new type of customer.

Sales management role plays help you in at least three areas; development of important sales management skills, career preparation, and classroom learning of important sales management concepts.

Sales Management Skills. These role plays will expose you to managerial dilemmas and allow you to experience the ramifications of your decisions. The role play process requires that you work in a small group, make realistic managerial decisions, and present and defend those decisions to the class. The role playing process will (1) enhance your oral communication skills and improve your ability to interact with peers, (2) provide you valuable exposure to sales and sales management concepts, and (3) allow you to exercise your decision-making skills.

Role plays are not substitutes for experience, but they can provide a good forum for discussions and a basis for correcting misconceptions. Role plays give you the opportunity to deal with sales management concepts from a fresh, non-textbook perspective. They provide insight into the excitement of the sales world as well as the challenges and opportunities that await the sales professional and manager. They address such real world problems such as ethics, recruiting, motivation, leadership, and interviewing. One important aspect of the role plays is that corporate politics frequently emerge in resolving the role play. You will find that in the work world, decisions are frequently driven as much by political concerns as by rational analysis.

Career Preparation. Role plays help students with limited experience in sales prepare for careers in sales management by demonstrating some of the opportunities and challenges of sales management. Role plays also help students overcome some of the negative stereotypes about personal selling and sales management. Many students, even marketing majors, have misconceptions about personal selling and sales management, some of which are caused by the portrayal of salespeople in the media and in fiction. Such fictional characters as Herb Tarlyk of *WKRP in Cincinnati,* Willy Loman in *Death of a Salesman,* Robin Williams in *Cadillac Man,* and Professor Harold Hill in *The Music Man* portray salespeople as fast-talking, hard-sell specialists with few morals. While isolated examples of these types of salespeople no doubt exist, most salesforces have become increasingly professional over the last twenty years. Firms have been forced to upgrade the skills of their salesforces as customer service and relationship building have become keys to attracting and retaining customers. Selling is the lifeblood of an organization. The effectiveness of the sales force and its management will, to a great extent, determine the overall success or failure of an organization.

Classroom Learning. Role plays provide an additional dimension to understanding sales management concepts and practice by enhancing textbook treatment of sales management topics and by stimulating class discussion. Topics that may seem dry in a textbook become much more interesting when demonstrated in a role play. The use of role plays in class is intended to stimulate classroom discussion. There should be lively debate over the solutions offered by the role play team since there are no hard-and-fast answers to the situations presented in the role play. Do not hesitate to critique the solutions to the role plays offered by your fellow students. In addition to critiquing the solution offered by the role play team, you are expected to offer your own analysis and solution to the role play. Be prepared to defend your solution as well.

The Role Plays

There are eleven role plays in this book. Several of the eleven role plays have multiple scenarios. Each role play deals with a different topic in sales management and has a different cast of characters.

Role Play 1: Aptitude. Characters: Sales Manager, Personnel Director, Prospective Employee.

Role Play 2: Interviewing. Characters: Good Interviewer, Bad Interviewer, Good Interviewee, Bad Interviewee.

Role Play 3: Training. Characters: Trainer, two new recruits, Sales Manager.

Role Play 4: Role Conflict. Characters: Salesperson, Customer, Sales Manager, Salesperson's spouse.

Role Play 5: Ethics. Characters: Sales Manager, Salesperson, Customer.

Role Play 6: Purchasing. Characters: Sales Manager, Salesperson, Customer.

Role Play 7: Territories. Characters: Sales Manager, Veteran Salesperson, Rookie Salesperson.

Role Play 8: Quota. Characters: District Manager, Sales Manager, Salesperson.

Role Play 9: Leadership. Characters: One or two Sales Managers, four Salespeople.

Role Play 10: Motivation. Characters: Regional Manager, Sales Manager, Salesperson.

Role Play 11: Compensation. Characters: Vice President of Sales, Regional Sales Manager, Prospective Employee.

For each role play, you will be provided with a description of the sales management situation and a description of the characters in the role play. The description of the sales management situation includes a discussion of three or four scenes involving a sales management concept, such as recruiting, leadership, motivation, or ethics, portrayed in a realistic way. Key dialogue elements are included for many of the scenes. The role plays typically contain the following scenes:

Scene 1: The first scene will introduce the characters and the basic problem to be examined and solved. This scene is quite detailed and generally includes some key dialogue. For example, the first scene of the quota role play has a sales manager and his/her district manager discussing quota problems in general. It also contains dialogue relating to problems with a particular salesperson who is not going to make quota.

Scene 2: The second scene will typically bring in a third character. Again, much of the basic dialogue or scenario is provided for the students. In the quota example, the sales manager meets with the salesperson to try to determine why quota is not being met and to examine what alternatives are available to help the salesperson.

Scene 3 (and possibly 4): In the third (and possibly fourth) scene, the situation is resolved. The role play group must present their solution of the situation. Very little direction is given for these scenes. Students can include whichever characters they wish and use any setting they feel is appropriate for the resolution of the situation. As you will see, the group's resolution of the role play determines which characters are included in the final scene and where the scene occurs.

Each role play also contains a description of the characters' personalities, educational and professional backgrounds, and "grapevine." The "grapevine" consists of corporate gossip about the characters' goals, work habits, and relationships with co-workers. There are some extra characters in the back of the book to allow students and faculty some alternatives to the existing characters.

Preparing for Role Plays: Directions for the Team Presenting the Role Play

The team presenting the role play group will consist of three to six people depending on the specific role play being performed. After determining who will play each character (if the instructor does not assign the roles), the first step is to *read the description* of the individual you will be portraying and attempt to "get into character." The role plays will be much more meaningful if each team member genuinely attempts to bring his/her character to life. The more realistic you can make the character, the more realistic your group's solution to the role play will be.

The second step is to *read the role play scenario and analyze the situation*. Begin by identifying the major problem represented in the role play. Once the group has identified a problem, the role play team members should begin to brainstorm to generate alternatives for dealing with the situation. You will find that there will usually be two or three alternatives that easily come to mind. Don't assume that those are the only alternatives or that the solution will emerge from those initial alternatives. It is important that you and your team spend time in considerable thought at this point. Remember, you and your team will have to defend your solution to the role play to the rest of the class.

The third step is to *create the role play*. A useful tool to organize the role play is a script (some instructors may require this step). Try to make the script as complete as possible. Include descriptions of the scenes and the individuals involved. The role plays are not lengthy, so the script should not require a great deal of dialogue.

Use the role play script to help you learn your character and how the characters in the role play interact. During the actual taping, however, do not read the script. You want to be as natural as possible. Your dialogue probably won't follow the script verbatim. Do not get anxious about your acting skills (or lack of them). Some of you will be naturals for role plays, others will never make Hollywood a career. The purpose of the role plays is to demonstrate good sales management techniques, not acting ability.

The fourth step is to present the role play. Instructors will either have the team present the role play live in front of class or on videotape. Your instructor will provide directions on presenting live role plays. In presenting taped role plays, different schools will have different equipment; therefore, it is not possible to give detailed, specific directions for making, editing, and exhibiting role play videotapes here. Be sure to get instructions from your instructor early in the semester as to what equipment will be available for making, editing, and exhibiting the videos.

A few tips might help make the presentations look more professional. First, scout out locations that will make the role play scenarios believable. If you have a scene in an office, use an office—a dorm room with a sign of a local beer emporium in the background is not very realistic. Second, use props to make the role play as realistic as possible. Props might include a model of the product, a mock-up of an ad, a price list, a copy of a letter, or whatever else you feel the characters in the role play would have in their possession. Third, rehearse the scene once or twice before taping. While it is not necessary for the acting to be professional, it is helpful if the actors know their lines and cues. You should also be alert to distracting mannerisms or inappropriate body language. Saying "um" twenty times during a scene can be very distracting. Further, weak dialogue and unrealistic solutions to the problem can be identified in practice and modified before shooting the final scene. A little practice can go a long way in making the role play appear professional.

The last step is to be creative. You have your alternatives and a final solution devised, but you also need to make the role play as entertaining (without being silly or crude) as possible. Realism and fun are both essential!

While the primary purpose of the role plays is to illustrate sales management issues, they will also allow you to watch yourself on videotape, perhaps for the first time. Watching yourself on tape can be a humbling experience. Keep in mind that the other members of the class must undergo the same process. It will help you keep a sense of proportion and humor if you happen to make a mistake.

Preparing for Role Plays: Instructions for the Class

Each member of the class should prepare the role play in basically the same manner as the role-play presenting team. For each role play, each class member must examine the issue/problem, create workable alternatives, examining the long-term consequences of each alternative; and then pick a solution and be prepared to defend it. Use the homework forms in the workbook for each role play.

Role Play Class Discussion

The class discussions that follow each role play should be entertaining, lively, and educational. Much of the value in the role plays is in the ensuing class discussion. Your class will typically be quick to criticize unworkable solutions, poor managerial style, and failure to consider long-term consequences of the solutions.

If the role plays are videotaped, your instructor will stop the tape at various points and ask for discussion. If the role plays are presented live, your instructor will probably wait until the end of a scene or the end of the entire role play before asking for discussion. This will avoid breaking the role players' train of thought during their presentation. During class discussion, do not be afraid of expressing your opinion. Remember, there isn't a correct answer. Your colleagues may or may not agree with your comment, but it will help elicit more discussion.

As far as the overall solutions are concerned, do not hesitate to voice agreement or objections to solutions posed by other class members. Many solutions may initially seem workable but may lead to bigger problems later on. Final solutions are not as important as the *thought* that each class member puts into analyzing the role play, and how well each class member defends his or her solution in class.

Look for and discuss realism in the role play. The presenting role players probably will do things that seem unrealistic for the business and management world. Examine management style as well as ultimate solutions. As you watch the role play, ask yourself such questions as: Would I want a manager like the one in the role play? How could the manager have better handled the situation or the person? If I were the manager, how would I have responded to the situation?

How to Use the Role Play Manual

Part II will present Pharmiceaux, (pronounced far-ma-co) Inc., a firm with $2.5 billion in sales of pharmaceuticals and hospital equipment for 1993. Each role play will be based on Pharmiceaux, Inc. A history of the company is presented as well as a detailed description of the product lines, market, industry, and competition. The organizational charts on pages 14 and 15 present a partial list of Pharmiceaux management and staff and show the formal lines of responsibility. Note that there are *two* organizational charts. One is for the Eastern District and the second is for the Western District. The genders of the characters are to be drawn from the two charts depending on how the roles were assigned to members of your group. For example, if a role play calls for a district manager, a sales manager, and a salesperson, the specific gender of each character is determined by whether a male or female on your team is playing the role.

The Pharmiceaux case also describes the sales organization including sales management issues such as recruiting, training, and compensation. You need to be familiar with Pharmiceaux's sales management practices. If the role play for the day is on training, for example, it is important that you review Pharmiceaux's training practices before preparing for the role play.

Each chapter in Part III will present a different role play. The chapter will begin with some basic information on the sales management topic that may be helpful in the role play. The role play scenario follows with a description of the scenes and the characters involved. The last few pages of each chapter contain three forms that will be used for the role play. The first form is a homework form that the instructor may require the day the role play is to be presented. The homework form may be turned in prior to the discussion of the role play. The second form, entitled "Evaluation of Role Players," is for your use in evaluating the role play. The evaluation form allows you to have input into the role play performance. Specifically, you are evaluating content (preparation, alternatives, solutions, and overall thoughtfulness), style (creativity, realism, professionalism, and extras), and the group's overall presentation. The last form is a note page to allow you to write down comments or points as you see them in the role play being discussed.

Over 100 characters appear throughout the book. The description of characters to be included appears at the end of each role play. Each character is given a background, including personality characteristics and performance evaluation. Each character has a male and female version depending on the composition of the role play team. At the end of the book are descriptions of alternative characters that might be used in different role plays.

PART II

CASE STUDY

Pharmiceaux, Inc.: Ethical Drug Division

PHARMICEAUX, INC.: ETHICAL DRUG DIVISION

Pharmiceaux History

Pharmiceaux, Inc. (pronounced far-ma-co) was founded in 1939 by William M. Russell, an established physician and weekend gourmet cook, in the garage of his home in Lafayette, Louisiana. Russell's mission for Pharmiceaux was "to contribute to the betterment of society through quality research and development of pharmaceutical products." In the years since, Pharmiceaux has enjoyed constant growth, interrupted only by a tragic laboratory fire in 1944, which halted operations for a ten-month period. While the company did go public in 1951, the Russell family continues to hold majority ownership. Pharmiceaux's involvement in all aspects of the pharmaceutical business—from research and discovery to development, marketing, and delivery—has allowed Pharmiceaux to build global brand identity.

Operational performance was superb in 1993 as Pharmiceaux attained its twentieth consecutive year of increased sales and earnings (see Tables 1.1 and 1.2 for Pharmiceaux's balance sheet and income statement). Operating income increased to over $744 million. Pharmiceaux continued to move forward strategically and to increase its investments in advanced technology and new customer service capabilities. Rapid change within the global health care market continues to create enormous opportunity, and Pharmiceaux continues to rise to the challenges presented. Pharmiceaux also made significant progress on its strategic priorities of concentrating resources more intensively on selected high-potential growth opportunities, and of shifting its mix of business toward areas that will prosper in the type of health care environment it will face in the next decade.

Pharmiceaux is composed of several major divisions. The largest, and oldest, organizational unit is the Ethical Drugs Division (EDD). This division develops, manufactures, and distributes prescription drugs to pharmacies and hospitals. Pharmiceaux's other divisions include Medical Equipment, International, and National Accounts and Telemarketing (see Figures 1.1 and 1.2 for organizational charts of the two Pharmiceaux regions).

EDD's Objective

EDD's objective for the 1990s is to be the worldwide best-cost producer in its core pharmaceutical business. EDD considers "best-cost" to mean having low costs relative to competitors while attaining levels of quality and value that set the standards for the industry. EDD believes that in health care, where lives depend on drugs, high quality and value standards are mandatory. This conviction motivates EDD in all aspects of its operation.

TABLE 1.1: Pharmiceaux Balance Sheets December 31, 1993 and 1992

	1993 (000s)		1992 (000s)	
ASSETS				
CURRENT ASSETS				
Cash and Cash Equivalents	$ 300,772	12.4%	$ 177,417	9.6%
Receivables	450,719	18.6	364,216	19.8
Inventories	258,681	10.7	210,682	11.4
Other Current Assets	555,068	22.9	400,894	21.8
TOTAL CURRENT ASSETS	1,565,240	64.6	1,153,209	62.6
PROPERTY AND EQUIPMENT	413,890	17.1	356,539	19.4
GOODWILL	175,377	7.2	104,915	5.6
OTHER ASSETS	267,450	11.1	227,742	12.4
	$2,421,957	100.0%	$1,842,405	100.0%
LIABILITIES AND STOCKHOLDERS' EQUITY				
CURRENT LIABILITIES				
Accounts Payable	$ 328,832	13.6%	$ 247,360	13.5%
Income Taxes Payable	51,736	2.1	23,030	1.2
Current Portion of Long-term Debt	80,000	3.3	100,000	5.4
Other Current Liabilities	339,151	14.0	193,420	10.5
TOTAL CURRENT LIABILITIES	799,719	33.0	563,810	30.6
DEFERRED INCOME TAXES	5,262	0.2	23,883	1.3
LONG-TERM DEBT, less current portion	189,407	7.8	129,651	7.0
OTHER LIABILITIES	37,706	1.6	56,296	3.1
	1,032,094	42.6	773,640	42.0
STOCKHOLDERS' EQUITY				
Common Stock	27,638	1.1	27,638	1.5
Additional Paid-in Capital	450,000	18.6	450,000	24.4
Retained Earnings *	912,225	37.7	591,127	32.1
	1,389,863	57.4	1,068,765	58.0
	$2,421,957	100.0%	$1,842,405	100.0%

* Dividends of $191,880 were paid in 1993.

EDD's Environment

EDD faces challenges in many aspects of its environment, including competition, government regulation, and changes in political and consumer preferences.

COMPETITION

The world ethical drug market increased 13 percent from 1992 to 1993. The industry is somewhat fragmented with the top ten companies in the world taking only 28 percent market share among them. There have been few changes in the

TABLE 1.2: Pharmiceaux Statements of Income Years Ended December 31, 1993 and 1992

	1993 (000s)		1992 (000s)	
NET SALES	$2,500,000	100.0%	$2,100,000	100.0%
COST OF SALES	578,744	23.1	535,662	25.5
GROSS PROFIT	1,921,256	76.9	1,564,338	74.5
SELLING, GENERAL, AND ADMINISTRATIVE EXPENSES	832,164	33.3	655,930	31.2
RESEARCH AND DEVELOPMENT	344,616	13.8	305,361	14.5
INCOME FROM OPERATIONS	744,476	29.8	603,047	28.7
OTHER INCOME	54,366	2.2	49,472	2.4
INTEREST EXPENSE	(13,153)	0.5	(11,942)	0.6
INCOME BEFORE INCOME TAXES	785,689	31.4	640,577	30.5
INCOME TAXES	272,711	10.9	225,183	10.7
NET INCOME	$ 512,978	20.5%	$ 415,394	19.8%
EARNINGS PER SHARE	$1.86		$1.50	

world ranking of pharmaceutical companies in 1993, with the top six occupying the same positions as in 1992. The principal reason for the stability in the ranking is that all these companies are devoting significant resources to developing new products to allow them to retain market share.

There is little doubt that the pharmaceutical industry has entered into a considerably tougher competitive global environment in the 1990s. Two major reasons account for this: (1) the large number of top-selling drugs expected to lose patent protection in the coming decade, and (2) the increasingly multinational nature of the market for drugs (see Table 1.3). Pharmiceaux EDD and other industry leaders are looking into market consolidation in order to counteract rising costs. However, thus far there have been few recent significant takeovers or mergers in the sector.

TABLE 1.3

Rank	Country	Value (billions)	% of World Market	% Growth from 1992 to 1993
1	USA	41.2	27	13
2	Japan	27.6	18	–1
3	Germany	12.5	8	8
4	France	11.5	8	10
5	Italy	11.0	8	17
6	UK	5.2	4	11
7	Spain	4.1	3	15
8	Canada	3.4	2	10
9	Brazil	2.8	2	45
10	South Korea	2.1	1	20
	Rest of World	28.6	19	13
	TOTAL	150.0	100	12

FIGURE 1.1: Pharmaceutical Division East Region

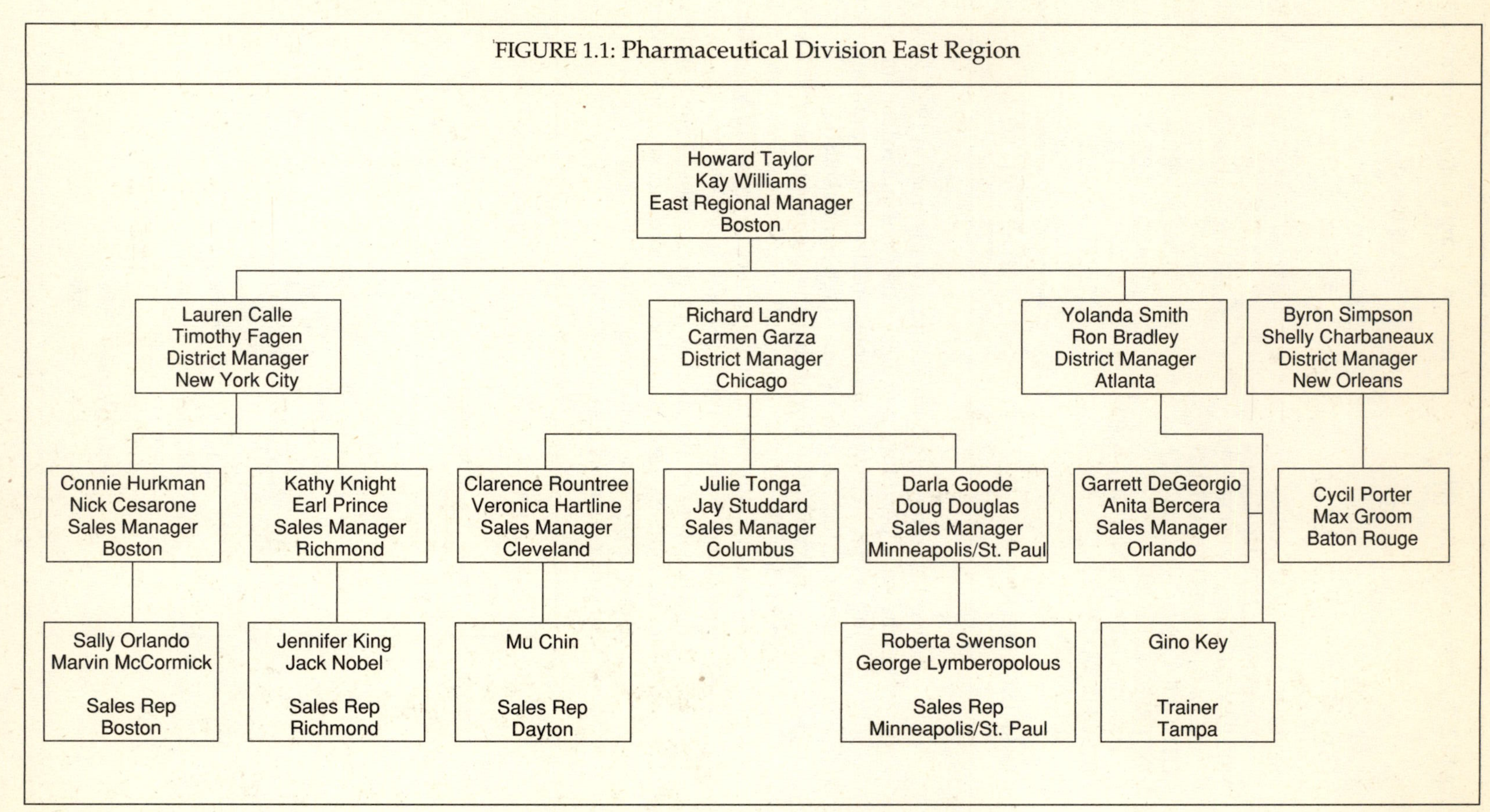

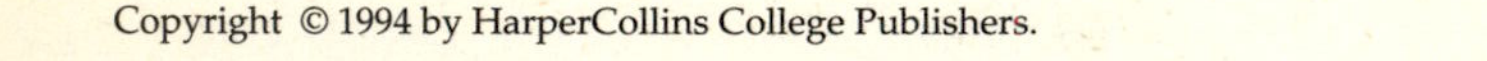

FIGURE 1.2: Pharmaceutical Division West Region

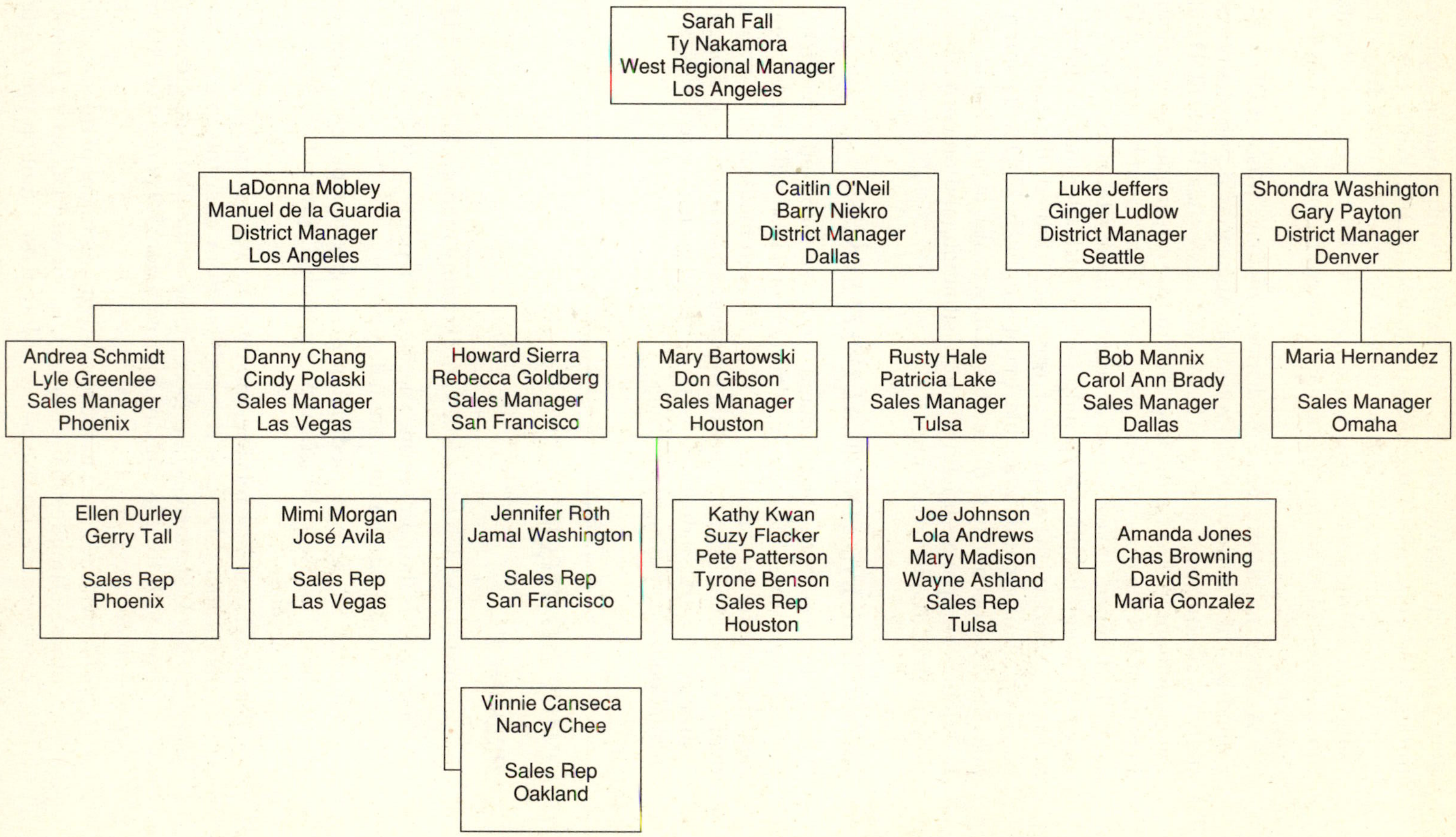

*If only one sales manager is used in the leadership role play have Johnson, Andrews, Madison and Ashland report to Houston.

GOVERNMENT REGULATION

EDD's major interaction with the government is with the drug approval process through the Food and Drug Administration (FDA). While this process has grown steadily more complex and time-consuming for most drugs, recent legislation speeds the process for drugs targeted for use by people with fatal or very rare diseases. EDD has maintained an excellent record with the FDA regarding drug approval.

Another regulatory issue is disposal of toxic waste. EDD was recently named by the Environmental Protection Agency as a potentially responsible party for cleanup costs at several hazardous waste sites. While EDD followed all the regulations in effect at the time the dumps were made, recent scientific findings point out the possible dangers to animal life posed by some of the chemical EDD dumped. Investigation of some of these sites is in a very preliminary stage. Although liability for cleanup costs of such sites may legally be imposed without regard to the quantity of waste contributed, the company believes, based on all information available, that it is unlikely EDD will incur any material costs in connection with these sites. EDD will also incur minimal costs in public relations, employee briefings on the situation, and on corrective actions to prevent this situation recurring.

CONSUMER AND POLITICAL PREFERENCES

Political tension and public demand are making cost-effective treatment a financial imperative. The growing elderly population will create large potential new markets for treatment of disease with high medical need among patients over 65. However, since most of these patients are on some form of government insurance, the drug industry must be extremely sensitive to changes in governmental policy on payment for drugs.

EDD's Marketing Strategy

PRODUCT

Five of the leading domestic drugs are currently manufactured by EDD.

Hydrazene is the number one vaccine for hepatitis B and contributes 18 percent of Pharmiceaux's annual sales.

Beatbetter xlt, a heart medication prescribed for patients with congenital heart disease, produces approximately 12 percent of Pharmiceaux's annual sales.

Pharmizeez, a muscle relaxer, is one of EDD's oldest and most widely-known medications. Despite competition from over-the-counter substitutes, sales of Pharmizees have been stable in the past nine quarters, varying from $197 to $198 million (approximately 7.9 percent of Pharmiceaux's annual sales).

Ulsir EX, which is used in the short-term treatment of duodenal ulcers and other gastrointestinal disorders, is one of EDD's two fastest growing new products on the market. More than 3 million prescriptions have been filled in the United States since its introduction in October 1989, and more than 500 clinical trials have been conducted involving more than 25,000 patients. Competitive analysis has shown that in its first three years on the market, Ulsir EX healed more patients in less time than its nearest competitor, resulting in greater cost efficiency for the insurer, and quicker recovery for the patient. One potential problem with this drug exists, as indicated by questionable results in tests on laboratory mice. While available endoscopic evaluations and histologic examinations of biopsy specimens from humans have not detected a risk from short-term exposure to Ulsir, EDD has allocated an unusually large portion of Ulsir's budget to continued research as a precautionary measure.

Pharmipro, the other new entry into the market, is an antibacterial agent which works through the inhibition of DNA synthesis. Pharmipro's release has been truly exciting to the pharmaceutical industry, as it demonstrates activity against organisms resistant to other antibacterial agents on the market. The market potential for Pharmipro is substantial as it can be prescribed for all patients 1 year and older.

Despite these market leaders, EDD faces a problem common to all drug manufacturers: rapidly escalating drug development costs. The most recent estimate stands at $230 million per drug brought to the market. Key factors in escalating development costs include increasing regulatory requirements and lengthening regulatory delays, as well as increasing technology and skilled labor costs in the actual research and development process. A long-term trend that is having a significant effect on research and development costs is the change in underlying technology used to produce pharmaceuticals. Biotechnology, rather than inorganic chemistry, is the new frontier for drug development. At the present, however, these technologies are not well understood and are extremely expensive, even by drug company standards. EDD hopes that increased therapeutic value of new drugs based on biotechnology may warrant premium prices to cover their higher costs.

PRICE

The issue of drug pricing causes industry leaders great concern. Pricing pressures are coming from both government and private buying organizations. This pressure is supported by an ever-increasing number of satisfactory drugs on the market for various disorders, which makes the task of innovation that much more complicated. It is increasingly difficult to obtain price increases that match the rate of inflation, or to introduce new drugs at prices that yield a satisfactory return on investment. EDD must also be sensitive to the increasing number of generic drugs entering the market. Until recently, generic drugs available have often been comparatively unsatisfactory. In the 1990s, however, increasing availability and quality of generic drugs will lead to their increased use. This will have a downward effect on drug pricing. EDD must also be sensitive to pricing issues related to the unification of Europe. It is currently thought that free flow of drugs across national borders in Western Europe will bring lower average prices since packaging and licensing regulations will become standardized.

DISTRIBUTION

EDD distributes its products directly to hospitals, clinics, and pharmacies. It is recognized as an industry leader in this area, constantly seeking new means of distributing products more effectively and efficiently. One method EDD uses to serve customers with maximum cost efficiency is a new program within the Ethical Drugs Division called LinkPlus, which provides "stockless" inventory management for hospitals and medical centers. The program streamlines the distribution of pharmaceuticals, significantly reducing costs in terms of time, storage, and handling. All customer service telephone lines are toll-free. Twenty-two major medical centers are currently using the program, and EDD expects participation by many more within the next two years.

PROMOTION

EDD's promotional program includes advertising in medical journals, sponsoring trade shows and guest lecturers for local medical societies, and public relations efforts aimed at regulators and legislators. Consistent with the rest of the industry, however, the bulk of EDD's promotional budget is spent on personal selling.

Sales Organization. EDD's salesforce is comprised of approximately 300 people (the organization chart indicates those who appear in a role play). EDD's sales organization is flat and decentralized, allowing managers wide latitude in making decisions in their markets without first obtaining corporate approval. The country is divided into two geographic regions, each with four districts. Each of the regional managers (East and West) has responsibility for activities in the four districts within his/her region. These responsibilities include setting and communicating quotas, coordinating monthly and quarterly reports, filing monthly progress reports, conducting performance evaluations, developing territorial budgets, and attending division meetings. Each district manager oversees six sales managers, and has authority for day-to-day operations within the district. The sales managers oversee six to eight sales representatives within the district and are also responsible for day-to-day operations.

The Salesforce. EDD's company-wide emphasis on total quality management and employee empowerment has resulted in the development of a salesforce whose commitment to the company is unmatched in the industry. This is evidenced by the fact that turnover among EDD's sales representatives is half that of its two closest competitors. EDD is renowned for its emphasis on employee development (both personal and career).

EDD's reputation within the industry is one of quality salesmanship. Representatives are for the most part known to be very professional and ethical in their business dealings. While some of their competitors are known for playing dirty by making deals "under the table" or by buying doctors' business with lavish gifts or perks, EDD policy strictly prohibits this type of conduct. Violations of EDD ethics policies are treated severely, and can result in termination.

Much of EDD's success is due to its company-wide dedication to customer involvement. EDD sales representatives are trained to be keenly aware of their customers to ensure that they are satisfied with the service they receive. This trade servicing approach is characterized by an emphasis on creative selling, providing detailed and accurate information, and servicing the customer whenever possible.

EDD's representatives must be efficient with their time. A typical sales representative's schedule begins early in the morning and involves several appointments throughout the day. Table 1.4 details a typical day.

Recruiting. With a 300-person salesforce, given EDD's historically high retention, EDD must hire approximately thirty new salespeople annually. These thirty new salespeople replace those who resign, retire, or are promoted. It is quite common for a salesperson to be promoted to sales management or to a marketing or general management position. EDD has made a practice of promoting from within whenever possible. Promoting from within mandates a particular emphasis on recruiting at the entry level. The majority of this entry-level recruiting is done through the top colleges and universities nationwide. In addition to campus recruiting, EDD works with private employment agencies, primarily in filling sales management positions. Due to the competitive nature of the pharmaceutical industry, the high cost of training, and EDD's emphasis on developing relationships with customers, EDD places great emphasis on recruiting individuals who show strong potential based on leadership capabilities, intelligence, and personal characteristics and experiences.

EDD's typical hire follows a six-step process:

Step 1: Job Position Request—A sales manager formally makes a request to the Personnel office for permission to fill a vacant sales position. Upon approval of request, the sales manager begins the interview process.

TABLE 1.4: A Typical EDD Sales Representative's Day

7:30–8:00	Review all correspondence by checking voice mail, reading mail, and reviewing electronic mail.
8:00–8:30	Print list of physicians in daily routing—review what was discussed last visit and what will be discussed today.
9:00–11:30	See 4 to 5 physicians. Review predetermined goal for discussion before each visit. Review names of office personnel. After each call, record details of discussion and goals for next visit. May schedule a lunch appointment.
11:30–12:00	Pick up food for lunch at physician's office. Drive to physician's office and prepare for lunch.
12:00–1:30	Doctor(s) and nurses have finished with patients and are ready for discussion over lunch. After lunch, record each discussion for future sales calls (details).
1:30–2:30	Make 2 to 3 pharmacy calls.
2:30–5:00	See 4 to 5 more physicians.
5:00–5:30	Clean car, reload samples for the next day.
5:30–6:00	Enter daily calls into computer and send via the phone line.

Step 2: Introductory Interview—Interviews are first held by sales managers, who are responsible for a preliminary evaluation of applicants, their resumes, and their applications. It is important to screen the applicant's knowledge of the company and to assess the fit between the prospective employee's goals and personality with those of the company.

Step 3: Management Interview—The second interview is typically held in the district manager's office. The prospective employee is given the opportunity to meet with several employees, including the regional manager whenever schedules permit.

Step 4: Aptitude Testing—EDD relies on a nationally known standardized aptitude test in order to compare various candidates. The series of tests requires about two hours of the applicant's time, and is usually administered as a part of the second round of interviews.

Step 5: Background Check and Analysis of the Aptitude Test—The screening process continues with a background check. This inquiry includes discussions with references provided by the applicant, researching the applicant's credit worthiness and driving record, and checking for any prior record of illegal drug use. Additionally, each candidate is given a numerical rating based on the previously administered aptitude test.

Step 6: Placement—Once a candidate has successfully completed the interviews and met set standards on the aptitude test, the recruiter extends an offer.

Compensation. Salespeople are compensated through a combination of salary and bonus. Entry-level salaries for newly hired sales representatives are comparable to EDD's largest competitor, as well as to entry-level sales positions with similar companies in other industries. It has been EDD's policy to give salary increases annually. These increases are given commensurate with cost of living increases and the merit achievements of the individual. In addition to annual salary, all employees are eligible for a year-end bonus, which is determined by the rating earned in the evaluation process. EDD employees receive a comprehensive compensation package with full health and dental benefits. EDD employees are eligible to participate in a company-wide 401K as regulated by the Internal Revenue Service.

All employees in the sales force are given a company car on beginning their territory sales. As an employee moves into management, car upgrades are added as a potential bonus/reward. Sales representatives and managers who are required to travel are reimbursed for miles at the rate set by the IRS.

In 1992 EDD announced a new employee incentive, offering employees a variety of stock options which are payable only after five years of service with the company.

Motivation. Motivation and recognition have always been cornerstones in EDD's Human Resources policies. This emphasis permeates every level of employee development and management, from recruitment through retirement. Employees are selected not only on the basis of their perceived capability, but also on the degree to which their goals, traits, needs, and wants are consistent with those of the organization. In addition, a great deal of time and resources are expended to maintain employee morale through various programs related to training, job review, and personal development.

To facilitate internal communication, managers are encouraged to operate under an "open door policy." In addition to this, written surveys are distributed to all employees, asking them to comment on product issues, corporate culture, or personal concerns.

Training. EDD devotes a great deal of money in training each year to ensure that its employees are professional and well educated on issues affecting its customers, the end users, and the industry as a whole. All of EDD's newly hired sales representatives are required to attend a four-week training institute in New Orleans as Phase I of a three-phase training program. During Phase I training, employees are paid salary plus all expenses. After one year in the field, sales representatives are eligible for Phase II, a two-week training course held at the corporate headquarters in Fort Worth, Texas. At a time deemed appropriate by the regional manager, the sales representative will be invited to participate in Phase III. This is a three-week course which prepares sales representatives for a position as a sales manager.

Quotas. Sales quotas for each district are set by upper management during the third quarter of each fiscal year for the next year. A national percentage increase in sales revenues is set in accordance with budgeted national sales projections. This percentage then becomes the average percentage quota for individual sales representatives.

Evaluation Process. All EDD employees are given annual performance reviews by their superiors. Evaluations are based on five critical issues: achievement of goals, professional conduct/work habits, territory management, product knowledge, and communication skills. Employees receive a rating (unsatisfactory, satisfactory, exceptional) in each area. Occasionally, sales managers and district managers are able to spend a day calling on customers with sales representatives. This on-the-job review gives both managers and representatives a unique opportunity to strengthen sales techniques.

EDD Use of Technology. EDD has historically positioned itself to be on the cutting edge of technology both in the development of new products and in the marketing of those products to the industry. The company has recently invested in information technology in order to strategically allocate its selling effort to current and future customers who will provide long-term growth opportunities. Salespeople use notebook-sized personal computers in their daily selling and account management activities. These PCs are used to input order information, generate invoices, and detail customer profile information. The notebooks also have software that enables the salesforce to maximize territory coverage through the use of a graphic display of customers within a city, county, or other geographical segment. Detailed time scheduling, prospecting, and servicing accounts are all possible through this software.

Information from the salesforce is linked with the central computers via modem and compiled with other customer-specific information. This database includes historic demand information and inventory counts. This process is performed in order to maintain detailed customer profiles that are aggregated and fed into models utilizing and revising market forecasts, as well as other internal and external market information. This information is shared with the Strategic Planning Department and other entities throughout the organization in order to analyze current and future opportunities.

PART III

THE ROLE PLAYS

ROLE PLAY 1

Aptitude

APTITUDE

Introduction

The recruiting process for salespeople can be long and multifaceted. Hiring firms will use a variety of recruiting techniques including resumes, interviews, aptitude tests (testing), references, and physicals. Many firms are now incorporating these activities through assessment centers. Assessment centers use multiple recruiting and selection techniques such as group discussion and interviews, presentations, role plays, and testing as part of the hiring process.

One common technique used in the hiring process is testing. There are several kinds of tests including: (1) intelligence, (2) general knowledge, (3) basic aptitude toward the job, (4) interests, and (5) personality. Intelligence tests are similar to the ACT or SAT college entrance examination in format. They are designed to determine basic intelligence levels and can be targeted toward specifics that relate to the job or industry.

General Knowledge tests are not directly related to intelligence levels but test knowledge of business events, basic marketing or sales information, and industry. The knowledge tests are typically included as part of a battery of tests.

Aptitude tests are used extensively in certain industries such as insurance, financial sales, and some technical industries. The purpose of the test is to determine whether applicants have a natural ability to perform the job. One of the myths of selling is that only certain people can make good salespeople. However, studies have not found that to be the case. Virtually anyone can be trained to be a good salesperson. However, there are people who have a natural aptitude for the job and, in theory, should be easier to train and should outperform their peers.

The last two types of tests examine an applicant's interests and personality. The interest tests ask such questions as: "Which would you rather do, read a book or talk to someone?" Sales companies tend to prefer extroverted personalities that are aggressive, enthusiastic, confident, and ambitious.

Companies that use tests tend to have policies regarding test administration, scoring, and use of results. Companies can run afoul of various hiring laws by incorrectly using tests as part of the hiring process. Tests are not designed to be automatic decision makers but rather are used as screening tools that are helpful in evaluating potential recruits.

In this role play, EDD is using tests to examine intelligence and basic sales aptitude. All applicants take the aptitude test and are expected to obtain a minimum score in order to continue the recruiting process. The problem occurs when a candidate who performs well on other steps of the hiring process (interview, resume) cannot seem to obtain the minimum score on the sales aptitude test. Role players must decide whether to allow the candidate to continue in the selection process. If so, what does the manager do with the applicants with low aptitude scores? Remember that all decisions the role players make have long-term consequences.

Aptitude Role Play

SCENARIO

EDD has experienced a turnover in a very important territory. Anita Bercera, the sales manager, has told Herbert McDonough, the personnel director, that EDD needs this position filled quickly. McDonough begins the recruiting process, filling out the required paperwork and preparing an ad to run in the weekend paper. Meanwhile, Tom Winchester walks into Bercera's office looking for a sales position. Tom has a very professional demeanor and Bercera's initial impression is favorable. For the past seven years Winchester has worked for a small pharmaceutical company and seems to have a good resume. His resume indicates that he has consistently made quota and has even won a sales award. Tom indicates that he left his previous company because of stagnation in his job. Tom appears to be a very pleasant individual and by the end of the interview, he has begun to achieve a rapport with Bercera.

SCENE 1

Scene 1 has Bercera talking with McDonough by phone. She summarizes the information about the open sales position and the importance of filling it quickly. As she hangs up, there is a knock on the door and Tom enters asking about a sales position. The scene fades and reopens as the interview is coming to a close 40 minutes later. Bercera is very impressed with Winchester's credentials and thinks that he may be the one to fill the open position. As the end of the interview approaches, Bercera mentions that she would like Winchester to fly to the district office in Atlanta for a second interview. Bercera explains that everyone is required to take a series of aptitude tests. Winchester, clearly showing some distress, states that he would prefer to skip the aptitude tests and let his experience, references, and abilities speak for themselves. Bercera laughs and says "you know, I always hated taking tests too, but EDD policy requires that all sales representatives must take the tests. However, I must admit that we have never had someone with your level of experience apply in recent memory. I'll check and maybe we can waive the test."

The first scene should end with the last couple of minutes of a favorable interview. It should be made clear to viewers that the interview has gone well and that Winchester seems to have all the right qualities to be a good sales rep.

The end of the interview should revolve around whether Winchester has to take the test. Reluctantly he agrees to it. The interview ends.

SCENE 2

Scene 2 involves Bercera and McDonough. Bercera raves about how impressed she is with Winchester and what an asset he would be to the company. McDonough replies, "Have you seen the results of his aptitude test? He didn't make the minimum passing score. Policy states that he is not to be hired!" This scene continues with discussion between the two on the merits of Winchester and the fairness of the policy.

Bercera and McDonough examine a number of alternatives; then they discuss the problems the chosen alternative will solve and what other problems may occur because of this alternative being implemented. After the discussion, the scene ends.

It is important that Bercera and McDonough defend their points of view in this scene. In addition, the discussion needs to review why aptitude tests are used as a selection tool. Finally, all alternatives need to be thoroughly examined.

SCENE 3

This is your scene! The role play team must decide what to do. This scene can include one, two, or all three characters. The location of the scene is also your choice. Attempt to defend your solution in the final scene.

Characters

1. Sales Manager: Anita Bercera or Garrett Degeorgio
2. Personnel Director: Herbert McDonough or Debbie Schrier
3. Applicant: Patti Gorman or Tom Winchester

Character Descriptions

Name: Patti Gorman		
Gender: F	**Age:** 29	**Marital Status:** Single
Education: BBA, State Tech		
Title: Applicant		
Employment History:	7 years with small pharmaceutical company in sales.	
Personality:	Very professional, excellent speaker, overachiever.	
Notes:	Well-groomed, professional, poised.	
Grapevine:	Does poorly on aptitude and standardized tests.	

Name: Tom Winchester		
Gender: M	**Age:** 29	**Marital Status:** Single
Education: BBA, Northwest State University		
Title: Applicant		
Employment History:	7 years with small pharmaceutical company in sales.	
Personality:	Very professional, excellent speaker, high achiever.	
Notes:	Tall, excellent dresser, seems professional, good experience.	
Grapevine:	Hates standardized tests.	

Name: Herbert McDonough		
Gender: M	**Age:** 46	**Marital Status:** Married
Education: BA, Emporia State; MS (Psychology), Kansas State		
Title: Personnel Director		**Office Location:** Fort Worth
Reports To:	VP, Personnel	
Employment History:	Started with company right out of school.	
Personality:	Very analytical, knowledgeable; lacks interpersonal skills, anal-retentive	
Notes:	Reads romance novels, has done a nice job as administrator.	
Grapevine:	Needs work on interpersonal skills.	

Name: Debbie Schrier		
Gender: F	**Age:** 41	**Marital Status:** Married
Education: BS in Human Resource Management, University of Wisconsin; also a CPA.		
Title: Personnel Director		**Office Location:** Fort Worth
Reports To:	VP, Personnel	
Employment History:	4 years with the company; legal secretary for 6 years; payroll for 2 years.	
Personality:	Bubbly, cheerful, never stressed.	
Notes:	Has a very lavish lifestyle; good administrator.	
Grapevine:	Recently reprimanded for unlawfully terminating an EDD employee.	

Name: Anita Bercera		
Gender: F	**Age:** 39	**Marital Status:** Single
Education: BBA, University of Colorado		
Title: Sales Manager		**Office Location:** Orlando
Reports To:	District Manager, Atlanta	
Employment History:	3 years with the company; 5 years experience in pharmaceutical sales; restaurant manager before that.	
Personality:	Stern but fair; office cutup—everyone's favorite manager; mothering.	
Notes:	Likes hiking and cooking; makes doll houses.	
Grapevine:	Good sixth sense.	

<table>
<tr><td colspan="3">Name: Garrett DiGeorgio</td></tr>
<tr><td>Gender: M</td><td>Age: 43</td><td>Marital Status: Married</td></tr>
<tr><td colspan="3">Education: BS (management), University of California at Davis</td></tr>
<tr><td colspan="2">Title: Sales Manager</td><td>Office Location: Orlando</td></tr>
<tr><td>Reports To:</td><td colspan="2">District Manager, Atlanta</td></tr>
<tr><td>Employment History:</td><td colspan="2">7 years with the company; 4 years previous experience in pharmaceutical sales.</td></tr>
<tr><td>Personality:</td><td colspan="2">Family man; mild mannered.</td></tr>
<tr><td>Notes:</td><td colspan="2">National champion skeet shooter; flies ultralight aircraft; gourmet cook.</td></tr>
<tr><td>Grapevine:</td><td colspan="2">Pushes his people hard, but is very supportive.</td></tr>
</table>

FORM 1

QUESTIONS FOR APTITUDE ROLE PLAY

NAME:

DATE:

CLASS SECTION:

QUESTION 1: What is the point of an aptitude test? How do companies use aptitude testing in recruiting?

QUESTION 2: How does company policy on the use of aptitude tests affect this hiring decision or any other hiring decision?

QUESTION 3: In this scenario, should Winchester have to take the aptitude test? Why or why not?

QUESTION 4: If Winchester fails to make the minimum score, what are the possible alternatives regarding his future with EDD? Consider the long-term consequences of your decision.

Alternative 1:

Consequences:

Alternative 2:

Consequences:

Alternative 3:

Consequences:

Alternative 4:

Consequences:

QUESTION 5: What solution would you have for this scenario? Defend your answer.

FORM 2

ROLE PLAY EVALUATION: APTITUDE

NAME:

DATE:

CLASS:

CONTENT:

1. Preparation	poor	1	2	3	4	5	outstanding
2. Alternatives	poor	1	2	3	4	5	outstanding
3. Solution	poor	1	2	3	4	5	outstanding
4. Thought	poor	1	2	3	4	5	outstanding

Comments:

STYLE:

1. Creativity	poor	1	2	3	4	5	outstanding
2. Realism	poor	1	2	3	4	5	outstanding
3. Professionalism	poor	1	2	3	4	5	outstanding
4. Extras	poor	1	2	3	4	5	outstanding

Comments:

OVERALL SCORE: poor 1 2 3 4 5 outstanding

NOTES AND COMMENTS ON THE APTITUDE ROLE PLAY

ROLE PLAY 2

Interviewing

INTERVIEWING

Introduction

The personal interview is the most widely used selection tool for salespeople. The resume, tests, and reference checks are all important recruiting tools, but none provide the level of insight that a personal interview can. The personal interview allows a recruiter to assess an applicant's ability to think on his/her feet, communication skills, career goals, and personality traits.

The interview process can vary widely depending on the company and the individual being interviewed. The interview process may consist of several interviews over time with different members of the hiring organization. The initial interview is generally designed to screen obviously unsuitable candidates, and usually takes a half hour to an hour. In college recruiting, this step can occur in the university placement office. Subsequent rounds might occur in a local or regional office, or possibly at the corporate headquarters. Later rounds are designed to get more in-depth information on the recruit and to expose the recruit to a variety of managerial personnel. The process can be lengthy and time-consuming for both the applicant and the company. Subsequent rounds might also include testing and "a day in the field."

There are several types of initial interviews. One of the most common is a structured interview. In structured interviews, all interviewees are asked the same predetermined questions, ensuring that all interviewees are treated equally. The second form of initial interview is an unstructured interview, which is the preferred method for more experienced recruiters. The unstructured method allows the recruiter to lead the interview in directions tailored to the particular interviewee. The last method of interviewing is known as a stress interview, in which the interviewer attempts to find out how the recruit will respond to pressure. The stress interview typically will include having the recruit sell the interviewer something such as a pencil. The stress technique can lead to hard feelings on the part of the recruit and is not recommended in all situations.

Interviews can bring out the best and the worst in people. Many interviewees are not well prepared for interviews. They have not done their homework for the interview and it becomes obvious early in the interview that they are not the candidate for this company. However, the same can be said for interviewers. Some are not prepared for the interview and it can be a very irritating experience for the interviewee. Interviewers are forbidden by law to ask certain types of questions. Table 2.1 provides a list of some of these illegal questions. Unfortunately, the illegal questions are in fact asked frequently in interviews.

This role play has two interviewers and two interviewees. In one scene, there is a well-prepared interviewer with an unprepared interviewee. There is also an unprepared interviewer with a prepared interviewee. There is a scene in which both participants are prepared. Table 2.2 provides the role players with a

TABLE 2.1: An Interview Guide for Affirmative Action Compliance Programs

Subject	Discriminatory Inquiries
Name:	The original name of an applicant whose name has been changed.
Sex	Make comments or notes unless sex is a BFOQ.*
Birthplace or residence	Birthplace of applicant or parents. Requirements that applicant submit a birth certificate.
Creed or religion	Religious affiliation, holidays observed, name of spiritual leader.
Race or color	Applicant's race, color of skin, eyes, or hair. Photographs are not permitted.
Marital status	Are you married, single, divorced, or engaged? Who lives with you?
Children	How many children do you have? Who cares for them? Do you plan to have children?
Age	How old are you?
Physical data	Height or weight.
Criminal record	Have you ever been arrested, convicted, or spent time in jail?
Military experience	Experience in armed forces other than U.S. Dates, conditions, or type of discharge. Reserve or draft status. Whereabouts during war years.
Housing	Do you own or rent your home? Do you live in an apartment? Do you live with your parents? Similar questions deal with length of residence, car owner ship, past garnishment of wages, and personal bankruptcy.
Citizenship	Any inquiry into whether the applicant is now or intends to become a U.S. citizen.
Education	Education may not be queried if it is not job related.
Organization	Any clubs, social fraternities, sororities, societies, lodges, or organizations to which the applicant belongs.
Language	Applicant's mother tongue, language learned at home, how the applicant acquired knowledge of a foreign language.
National origin	Applicant's lineage, national origin, or that of parents or spouse.
Relatives	Name and/or address of any relative.

*Bona fide occupational qualification.

Source: L. Chonko, B. Enis, J. Tanner, *Managing Salespeople* (Boston: Allyn and Bacon, 1992), 410.

TABLE 2.2: Negative Factors Identified during the Employment Interview that Frequently Lead to Rejection of Applicants

1. Poor appearance
2. Overbearing, overaggressive, conceited attitude
3. Inability to express self clearly; poor voice, diction, grammar
4. Lack of career planning; no purpose or goals
5. Lack of interest and enthusiasm; a passive, indifferent manner
6. Lack of confidence and poise; nervousness
7. Failure to participate in extra-curricular activities
8. Overemphasis on money, interest in "best dollar": offer
9. Poor scholastic record
10. Unwillingness to start at the bottom; the expectation of too much too soon
11. Evasiveness; failure to be clear about unfavorable factors in record
12. Lack of tact
13. Lack of maturity
14. Lack of courtesy
15. Condemnation of past employers
16. Lack of social understanding
17. Marked dislike for schoolwork
18. Lack of vitality
19. Failure to look interviewer in the eye
20. Limp, fishy handshake
21. Indecision
22. Unhappy married life
23. Friction with parents
24. Little sense of humor
25. Sloppy, poorly prepared application blank
26. Evidence of merely shopping around for a job
27. Desires job for short time only
28. Lack of knowledge in field of specialization
29. No interest in company or industry
30. Emphasis on who he knows; name dropping
31. Unwillingness to go where company may want to send him
32. Cynical attitude
33. Low moral standards
34. Laziness
35. Intolerance; strong prejudice
36. Narrow interests
37. Evidence of wasted time
38. Poor handling of personal finances
39. No interest in community activities
40. Inability to take criticism
41. Lack of appreciation of the value of experience
42. Radical ideas
43. Tardiness (to interview) without good reason
44. Failure to express appreciation for interviewer's time
45. Failure to ask questions about the job
46. Indefinite responses to questions

Source: C. Futrell, *Sales & Management* (New York: Holt, Rinehart & Winston, 1981), 223.

list of 46 negative factors identified during interviews. As the bad interviewee, you might want to incorporate as many of these negatives as possible.

Interviewing Role Play

SCENARIO

Recently, EDD has had an opening in a midwest territory due to a retirement of Mu Chin who was with EDD for 30 years. EDD has typically let the area sales manager do introductory interviews (see pages 19 and 20 of Pharmiceaux case) with soon-to-be-graduates from universities in or near the open territory.

Richard Landry has informed two of his managers to begin recruiting at universities in Ohio. Veronica Hartline has been a manager for seven years and has hired over 20 sales reps in that time period. She is very polished and is completely at ease interviewing. Hartline's interview policy has always been to learn as much as possible about the recruit without making him or her feel uncomfortable.

Jay Studdard has recently been promoted to sales manager and is still a little overwhelmed with the new responsibilities. He has never interviewed anyone before and has not had a chance to attend the human resources seminar that EDD holds every year to teach managers how to conduct interviews. Studdard is 27 years old and impressed with himself. This arrogance will come across in the interview as will some ignorance as to what cannot be asked in an interview. The last scene requires the sales managers to meet, discuss the recruits, and recommend one of the interviewees for additional interviews.

SCENE 1

The first scene features Hartline and Brian Allen Lazarko, an interviewee who is totally unprepared for the interview. Hartline must suffer through an absolutely horrible interview. The bad interviewee is to do the worst interview possible. Lazarko should include as many of the negative factors from Table 2.2 as possible. This interview should be very entertaining while showing the class what not to do in an interview.

SCENE 2

The second scene features Studdard, who is not well prepared for the interview, and Aimee Breaux. Studdard will ask illegal questions and questions that appear to be a bit off-the-wall (see Table 2.1 for examples of illegal questions). Breaux needs to maintain her composure and do the best she can in a bad interview.

SCENE 3

The third scene features Hartline with Aimee Breaux, a well-prepared interviewee. The interviewee has done her homework on EDD and seems very professional. Breaux should try to do as good an interview as possible. (Note: Do not worry about being perfect in the interview. Obviously, mistakes occur in every interview. The class will discuss what Breaux did well and what she could have improved on).

SCENE 4

The fourth scene features Hartline and Studdard. They must decide which of the two interviewees, Breaux or Lazarko, to recommend for the second step of the hiring process (the management interview). Studdard should walk into Hartline's office saying, "I just finished the interview with Lazarko. A little unorthodox, but lots of enthusiasm!" The rest of the scene should be a discussion between the two managers as to whether they should recommend Lazarko or Breaux (or both, or neither) for the second stage of the hiring process. The scene should conclude with a definite recommendation (pro or con) for Breaux and Lazarko.

Characters

1. Experienced Sales Manager: Veronica Hartline or Clarence Rountree
2. Inexperienced Sales Manager: Jay Studdard or Julie Tonga
3. Good Interviewee: Alex Minyard or Aimee Breaux
4. Bad Interviewee: Brian Allen Lazarko or Darlene Dauer
5. District Manager: Richard Landry or Carmen Garza

Character Descriptions

Name: Veronica Hartline		
Gender: F	**Age:** 32	**Marital Status:** Single
Education: BA, University of Mississippi		
Title: Sales Manager		**Office Location:** Cleveland
Reports To:	District Manager, New York	
Employment History:	Hired straight out of school; has been a manager for 5 years.	
Personality:	Easygoing but hard-working; detail-oriented.	
Notes:	Wants to mentor young females in the company. Spends long-hours at the office. Likes movies.	
Grapevine:	Wants to relocate back to the deep South.	

Name: Richard Landry			
Gender: M	**Age:** 54	**Marital Status:** Married	
Education: BA, Tulane; MBA, Harvard			
Title: District Manager, Chicago		**Office Location:** Chicago	
Reports To:	East Regional Manager		
Employment History:	Sales with competitor for 3 years, sales manager for 2 years, quit to get MBA; Pharmiceaux sales manager for 5 years; district manager for 10 years.		
Personality:	Cooperative, persevering, poised, good sense of humor, energetic.		
Notes:	2 children, both in college; had open-heart surgery 2 years ago.		
Grapevine:	Told to cut back stress.		

Name: Carmen Garza			
Gender: F	**Age:** 41	**Marital Status:** Married	
Education: BS, Jackson State; MBA, Georgetown			
Title: District Manager, Chicago		**Office Location:** Chicago	
Reports To:	East Regional Manager		
Employment History:	Taught elementary school for 6 years; sales with competitor for 3 years; quit to get MBA. EDD sales for 3 years, sales manager for 5 years; district manager for 2 years.		
Personality:	Great sense of humor; down-to-earth; driven; well-liked.		
Notes:	Said to have photographic memory; 3 children, oldest at the University of California, Irvine.		
Grapevine:	May leave for state politics.		

Name: Clarence Rountree		
Gender: M	**Age:** 48	**Marital Status:** Married
Education: BS, Auburn		
Title: Sales Manager		**Office Location:** Cleveland
Reports To:	District Manager, New York	
Employment History:	Has been a manager for 17 years, came to Pharmiceaux from a competitor.	
Personality:	Very sensitive to the needs of his people; good sense of humor, likeable	
Notes:	One of the best recruiters in the country; likes recruiting college students; coaches Little League.	
Grapevine:	May take a staff position in Human Resources.	

Name: Julie Tonga		
Gender: F	**Age:** 26	**Marital Status:** Married
Education: BBA, State Tech		
Title: Sales Manager		**Office Location:** Columbus, OH
Reports To:	District Manager, Chicago	
Employment History:	Been with company for 6 years; hired originally as an intern.	
Personality:	Intelligent, driven, little sense of humor.	
Notes:	Career-oriented; wants to be in upper management soon. Not well-liked by some of her peers.	
Grapevine:	Needs some maturity.	

<table>
<tr><td colspan="3">Name: Jay Studdard</td></tr>
<tr><td>Gender: M</td><td>Age: 27</td><td>Marital Status: Single</td></tr>
<tr><td colspan="3">Education: BBA, Northwest State</td></tr>
<tr><td colspan="2">Title: Sales Manager</td><td>Office Location: Columbus, OH</td></tr>
<tr><td>Reports To:</td><td colspan="2">District Manager, Chicago</td></tr>
<tr><td>Employment History:</td><td colspan="2">5 years with the company, 6 months as a manager.</td></tr>
<tr><td>Personality:</td><td colspan="2">Big ego—impressed with his own abilities; intelligent.</td></tr>
<tr><td>Notes:</td><td colspan="2">Wants to be a CEO and to get there as soon as possible. Loyal to himself first.</td></tr>
<tr><td>Grapevine:</td><td colspan="2">Needs some seasoning; not sure of his managerial abilities.</td></tr>
</table>

<table>
<tr><td colspan="3">Name: Alex Minyard</td></tr>
<tr><td>Gender: M</td><td>Age: 22</td><td>Marital Status: Single</td></tr>
<tr><td colspan="3">Education: BS in Marketing, Ohio State University</td></tr>
<tr><td colspan="3">Title: Recruit</td></tr>
<tr><td>Employment History:</td><td colspan="2">Student body President; interned with a Fortune 500 company.</td></tr>
<tr><td>Personality:</td><td colspan="2">Aggressive and confident. Organized, high energy, good sense of humor.</td></tr>
<tr><td>Notes:</td><td colspan="2">Highly sought after by several companies; Pharmiceaux is very interested in him.</td></tr>
<tr><td>Grapevine:</td><td colspan="2">Potential fast-track candidate.</td></tr>
</table>

Name: Aimee Breaux (pronounced "Bro")		
Gender: F	**Age:** 21	**Marital Status:** Single, engaged
Education: BS in Marketing, Ohio State University		
Title: Recruit		
Employment History:	Part-time sales experience; graduates in 1 month. Studied in Europe one summer.	
Personality:	Vivacious, intelligent, class leader.	
Notes:	Daughter of a doctor. Her professors ranked her as the best marketing student of the year.	
Grapevine:	Potential fast-track candidate.	

Name: Darlene Dauer		
Gender: F	**Age:** 21	**Marital Status:** Single
Education: Ohio State University		
Title: Student		
Employment History:	No full-time work experience.	
Personality:	Disorganized; very immature.	
Notes:	No serious goals or plans; poor student.	
Grapevine:	Is searching for a job to satisfy her parents.	

Name: Brian Allen Lazarko		
Gender: M	**Age:** 23	**Marital Status:** Single
Education: Ohio State University		
Title: Student		
Employment History:	Ran a backyard lemonade stand.	
Personality:	Disorganized; no goals; is unrealistic.	
Notes:	Low grades, class clown; doesn't know what he wants, except high pay	
Grapevine:	Probably can't pass the drug test.	

Name: Mu Chin		
Gender: M	**Age:** 65	**Marital Status:** Married
Education: BA, National University of Singapore		
Title: Senior Sales Rep		**Office Location:** Dayton, OH
Reports To:	Sales Manager, Dayton	
Employment History:	Been with Pharmiceaux since the company's beginning; is now retiring.	
Personality:	Well-respected, "Grandfather" for the organization; hard worker.	
Notes:	Retiring; will have honorary title	
Grapevine:	May be used as a part-time trainer/consultant.	

FORM 1

QUESTIONS FOR INTERVIEWING ROLE PLAY

NAME:

DATE:

CLASS SECTION:

QUESTION 1: What are the characteristics of a good interviewer?

QUESTION 2: What actions can the interviewer and interviewee take to get the interview started in a positive direction?

QUESTION 3: How should an interviewee handle questions that may be discriminatory?

QUESTION 4: How well did the interviewer do in learning important facts about the candidates?

FORM 2

ROLE PLAY EVALUATION: INTERVIEWING

Good Interviewer/Bad Interviewee

NAME:

DATE:

CLASS:

CONTENT:

1. Preparation	poor	1	2	3	4	5	outstanding
2. Alternatives	poor	1	2	3	4	5	outstanding
3. Solution	poor	1	2	3	4	5	outstanding
4. Thought	poor	1	2	3	4	5	outstanding

Comments:

STYLE:

1. Creativity	poor	1	2	3	4	5	outstanding
2. Realism	poor	1	2	3	4	5	outstanding
3. Professionalism	poor	1	2	3	4	5	outstanding
4. Extras	poor	1	2	3	4	5	outstanding

Comments:

OVERALL SCORE:	poor	1	2	3	4	5	outstanding

FORM 2

ROLE PLAY EVALUATION: INTERVIEWING

Good Interviewer/Good Interviewee

NAME:

DATE:

CLASS:

CONTENT:

1. Preparation	poor	1	2	3	4	5	outstanding
2. Alternatives	poor	1	2	3	4	5	outstanding
3. Solution	poor	1	2	3	4	5	outstanding
4. Thought	poor	1	2	3	4	5	outstanding

Comments:

STYLE:

1. Creativity	poor	1	2	3	4	5	outstanding
2. Realism	poor	1	2	3	4	5	outstanding
3. Professionalism	poor	1	2	3	4	5	outstanding
4. Extras	poor	1	2	3	4	5	outstanding

Comments:

OVERALL SCORE: poor 1 2 3 4 5 outstanding

FORM 2

ROLE PLAY EVALUATION: INTERVIEWING

Bad Interviewer/Good Interviewee

NAME:

DATE:

CLASS:

CONTENT:

1. Preparation	poor	1	2	3	4	5	outstanding
2. Alternatives	poor	1	2	3	4	5	outstanding
3. Solution	poor	1	2	3	4	5	outstanding
4. Thought	poor	1	2	3	4	5	outstanding

Comments:

STYLE:

1. Creativity	poor	1	2	3	4	5	outstanding
2. Realism	poor	1	2	3	4	5	outstanding
3. Professionalism	poor	1	2	3	4	5	outstanding
4. Extras	poor	1	2	3	4	5	outstanding

Comments:

OVERALL SCORE: poor 1 2 3 4 5 outstanding

FORM 2

ROLE PLAY EVALUATION: INTERVIEWING

Managers' Discussion of Breaux and Lazarko

NAME:

DATE:

CLASS:

CONTENT:

1. Preparation	poor	1	2	3	4	5	outstanding
2. Alternatives	poor	1	2	3	4	5	outstanding
3. Solution	poor	1	2	3	4	5	outstanding
4. Thought	poor	1	2	3	4	5	outstanding

Comments:

STYLE:

1. Creativity	poor	1	2	3	4	5	outstanding
2. Realism	poor	1	2	3	4	5	outstanding
3. Professionalism	poor	1	2	3	4	5	outstanding
4. Extras	poor	1	2	3	4	5	outstanding

Comments:

OVERALL SCORE: poor 1 2 3 4 5 outstanding

NOTES AND COMMENTS ON THE INTERVIEWING ROLE PLAY

Good Interviewer/Bad Interviewee

NOTES AND COMMENTS ON THE INTERVIEWING ROLE PLAY

Good Interviewer/Good Interviewee

NOTES AND COMMENTS ON THE INTERVIEWING ROLE PLAY

Bad Interviewer/Good Interviewee

ROLE PLAY 3

Training

TRAINING

Introduction

Training can take a number of forms and methods. A large percentage of companies have no formal training program but rather rely on OJT (on-the-job training). The new employee will begin in their territory with some supervisory assistance and training. Many companies feel that the best way for new salespeople to learn is "to do." Obviously, the direct, out-of-pocket expenses of OJT are much less than the formalized classroom training that EDD uses.

The arguments for a formalized classroom training program are numerous. First, many companies' products are technical or so numerous that some form of training is necessary to acquaint the new salesperson with the intricacies of the line. Second, a number of companies (particularly Fortune 500) want to encourage new hires to become enculturated to the way the firm does business, and believe this can be more easily accomplished in a formal classroom setting. The purpose of this enculturation is to make the newly hired sales employees feel a part of the company "family." The orientation of new hires is designed to eliminate the new job "jitters." Orientation may also familiarize the new employee with the "who's who" of the company. Last, the socialization process allows a class to build a comraderie that will remain with new employees and their peers throughout their career.

There are other practical reasons for formalized training such as teaching how to sell the company way, teaching the value and necessity of customer relations, and decreasing turnover by better informing employees.

Formalized training programs vary in length. The norm is somewhere between two weeks and three months. The location of a training center also varies. Many companies will train in a national training center located at a single site. These types of training centers tend to have a "class" of students that train together, with new classes beginning periodically throughout the year. Other organizations have continual classes where training is ongoing and may include only a handful of people at any one point in the training. In other words, new salespeople are immediately sent to training regardless of whether there are others that need to be trained. Other companies have regional sales centers where training occurs for new people in that region. Most formalized training will end with the trainee's sales manager spending some time in the field with the new employee.

Classroom training can be an important beginning to a salesperson's career. The days are long and some classes or homework assignments extend into the evening hours. Rookie salespeople sometimes mention that sales training is as rigorous as anything they have done in school up to that point. Training typically involves intense study and frequent testing. The trainees may find that they have never read so much material in their lives (particularly if their firm sells highly technical products).

EDD conducts four weeks of intensive training in New Orleans. EDD trainees must have a crash course on the human body, be familiar enough with medicine that they can have meaningful dialogue with doctors, and be experts on EDD products. One trainee was overheard to say, "I feel like I just finished Med school."

The role play involves two sales trainees and a sales trainer. The first scenario concerns an event that was added to the schedule after the apparent completion of the program. The two trainees will react differently to the changes. In the second scenario, the two trainees receive their territory assignments. One of the trainees is told she will receive additional training which will result in a delay in her territory assignment.

Training

SCENARIO A

Amanda Jones and David Smith are both new recruits who are currently attending EDD's four-week training institute in New Orleans. Both are based in Dallas and will return to Dallas to receive their territory assignments on completion of the training period.

The trainees are scheduled to fly back to their home office early Saturday morning. Bill Nelson, the executive in charge of training, calls Amanda and David on Friday, the last day of training, to tell them that the company is holding a wine and cheese party to celebrate the conclusion of training. Amanda is upset because the training schedule indicated that the training session was over Friday at 5 o'clock and she has friends and parents driving in from Baton Rouge to see her that night. She hasn't seen these friends in over three years. She thinks to herself that she may just have to "cut" this company function.

SCENE 1

The first scene has Nelson talking to Amanda and David about their successful completion of the training function. He compliments them on their work during training. The scene needs to have Nelson summarize the above scenario information emphasizing that this is the last day of the training period and that they have been in New Orleans for the past four weeks. Nelson concludes with "I realize that the party was not on the schedule, but we think the session will be beneficial and we're hoping some company executives will show." Amanda asks in a somewhat sarcastic tone why the party was not on the schedule. Nelson's reply is that it was a last minute addition. Nelson again congratulates the twosome and leaves stating, "I'll see you two at the party."

SCENE 2

This scene is a continuation of Scene 1 beginning with Amanda vehemently complaining to David about this change in schedule and how she has friends coming in from Baton Rouge. Amanda says, "It was rude, rude, rude!" David tries to show her some of the advantages of attending the party, but Amanda is concerned about seeing her friends. The scene can end with her planning not to attend, briefly attending, or attending the entire event.

SUMMARY

The class discussion for this role play should focus on who is right and who is wrong in this role play. Scene 2 needs to focus on why the party is being held and if there are consequences to not attending the party. Think about this! There is more to this than you might think at first glance.

SCENARIO B

Monday morning after the training program Bob Mannix has called Dave and Amanda to his office. He meets with Dave and Amanda separately to give them their territory assignments. He gives Dave his assignment and tells him to begin immediately. He tells Amanda she can begin only after receiving some additional training on dealing with sexual harassment. After talking with Dave, Amanda feels that she is being discriminated against since she is not allowed to begin working her territory as quickly as Dave and goes in to Mannix and complains.

SCENE 1

Mannix calls Dave in first, welcomes him and informs him that beginning Tuesday, he will be covering a North Dallas territory by himself for a two-week period and then will come back to headquarters for a week of debriefing. David is obviously delighted. Mannix dismisses Dave and calls in Amanda. Mannix tells Amanda that EDD is equally as impressed with her. However, Amanda will be required to stay for an extra day of additional training. Further, for the first couple of weeks, she will have a manager ride with her in her territory. Amanda, rather perturbed, asks "Why? I spoke to Dave in the hall and you are not requiring him to attend extra training, nor is a manager going to be riding with him." Mannix explains that they have had problems in the past with customers harassing their female reps and have in fact recently lost a rep and some accounts because of "problems." Mannix says, "We want our female reps to be prepared to handle customers who may not have enlightened attitudes about female sales representatives." Amanda exclaims, "It's not fair! David isn't getting this 'extra' treatment. Make him stay too. It's blatant discrimination. I've been around and I can take care of myself!"

SCENE 2

The second scene should be your perception of what should have occurred after the first scene. How would you have handled the situation if you were Mannix?

Characters

1. Trainee: Amanda Jones or Chas Browning
2. Trainee: David Smith or Maria Gonzales
3. Trainer: Debra Joyner or Bill Nelson
4. Sales Manager: Bob Mannix or Carol Ann Brady

Character Descriptions

Name: Debra Joyner		
Gender: F	**Age:** 42	**Marital Status:** Divorced twice
Education: BA, Villanova		
Title: Trainer		**Office Location:** New Orleans
Reports To:	Personnel Director	
Employment History:	Has been with the company for 15 years; 10 years as a sales rep.	
Personality:	Outgoing, friendly; a good motivator.	
Notes:	Recently divorced; likes to travel, enjoys outdoor activities; is a good teacher.	
Grapevine:	Burnout from sales position led to job as a trainer.	

Name: Bill Nelson		
Gender: M	**Age:** 40	**Marital Status:** Married
Education: BA, Indiana University		
Title: Trainer		**Office Location:** New Orleans
Reports To:	Personnel Director	
Employment History:	Has been with Pharmiceaux for 12 years; 8 years as a sales rep.	
Personality:	Outgoing, energetic, good sense of humor, motivational.	
Notes:	Works with children's charities; athletic; likes sailing, coaches little league; loves training.	
Grapevine:	May have suffered from sales rep burnout leading to this job as a trainer.	

Name: Amanda Jones		
Gender: F	**Age:** 26	**Marital Status:** Single
Education: BA, North State Tech		
Title: Sales Trainee		**Office Location:** Dallas
Reports To:	Trainer	
Employment History:	3 years in retail.	
Personality:	Uptight; self-serving and demanding; self-assured.	
Notes:	Did well in training; does not appear to be a company person yet; likes the nightlife.	
Grapevine:	May have an attitude problem.	

<table>
<tr><td colspan="3">Name: Chas Browning</td></tr>
<tr><td>Gender: M</td><td>Age: 27</td><td>Marital Status: Single</td></tr>
<tr><td colspan="3">Education: BBA, State University</td></tr>
<tr><td colspan="2">Title: Sales Trainee</td><td>Office Location: Dallas</td></tr>
<tr><td>Reports To:</td><td colspan="2">Trainer</td></tr>
<tr><td>Employment History:</td><td colspan="2">Worked in father's computer sales business.</td></tr>
<tr><td>Personality:</td><td colspan="2">"Mr. Personality"—arrogant, rude, demanding.</td></tr>
<tr><td>Notes:</td><td colspan="2">Did well in training; not a company person yet; not a team player; enjoys the nightlife.</td></tr>
<tr><td>Grapevine:</td><td colspan="2">Attitude/personality may be a problem.</td></tr>
</table>

<table>
<tr><td colspan="3">Name: David Smith</td></tr>
<tr><td>Gender: M</td><td>Age: 23</td><td>Marital Status: Married</td></tr>
<tr><td colspan="3">Education: BS, South Florida</td></tr>
<tr><td colspan="2">Title: Sales Trainee</td><td>Office Location: Dallas</td></tr>
<tr><td>Reports To:</td><td colspan="2">Trainer</td></tr>
<tr><td>Employment History:</td><td colspan="2">Fresh out of school.</td></tr>
<tr><td>Personality:</td><td colspan="2">Level-headed, hard-working, mature, and aggressive.</td></tr>
<tr><td>Notes:</td><td colspan="2">Recently married; company team player; likes tennis.</td></tr>
<tr><td>Grapevine:</td><td colspan="2">Fast-tracker.</td></tr>
</table>

Name: Maria Gonzales		
Gender: F	**Age:** 24	**Marital Status:** Single
Education: BBA, Northwestern		
Title: Sales Trainee		**Office Location:** Dallas
Reports To:	Trainer	
Employment History:	Fresh out of school.	
Personality:	Aggressive, mature; good leadership qualities	
Notes:	Team player; success-driven, self-starter; soccer player.	
Grapevine:	Fast-tracker.	

Name: Bob Mannix		
Gender: M	**Age:** 45	**Marital Status:** Widower
Education: BBA, LSU Executive MBA; SMU		
Title: Sales Manager		**Office Location:** Dallas
Reports To:	District Manager, Dallas	
Employment History:	Entrepreneur 7 years, sales with Pharmiceaux for 8 years, manager 7 years.	
Personality:	Out-going, adventurous, very competitive.	
Notes:	Drives race cars, parachutes, scuba diver.	
Grapevine:	May retire early if not promoted.	

Name: Carol Ann Brady		
Gender: F	**Age:** 43	**Marital Status:** Married
Education: BS, Stanford		
Title: Sales Manager		**Office Location:** Dallas

Reports To:	District Manager, Dallas
Employment History:	7 years with Pharmiceaux, 3 years leave of absence, the past 10 years back with Pharmiceaux, the last 3 as sales manager.
Personality:	Perky, vivacious, friendly.
Notes:	Second marriage, 6 children, the oldest beginning college.
Grapevine:	Very steady manager. Not looking for promotion.

FORM 1

QUESTIONS FOR TRAINING ROLE PLAY

NAME:

DATE:

CLASS SECTION:

QUESTION 1: What might be the purpose(s) of a wine and cheese party at the conclusion of a training program?

QUESTION 2: Was the company wrong in not scheduling the party on the trainees' agenda? Should EDD have given the recruits more notice?

QUESTION 3: Regarding the party attendance, is Amanda in the wrong? Why or why not?

QUESTION 4: What realistic alternatives does Amanda have regarding the party?

Alternative 1:

Consequences:

Alternative 2:

Consequences:

Alternative 3:

Consequences:

Alternative 4:

Consequences:

QUESTION 5: What realistic alternatives does Amanda have regarding the extra training and the accompanying manager?

Alternative 1:

Consequences

Alternative 2:

Consequences:

Alternative 3:

Consequences:

Alternative 4:

Consequences:

QUESTION 6: If you were management in the first role play, how would you have handled the party differently?

FORM 2

ROLE PLAY EVALUATION: TRAINING (A)

NAME:

DATE:

CLASS:

CONTENT:

1. Preparation	poor	1	2	3	4	5	outstanding
2. Alternatives	poor	1	2	3	4	5	outstanding
3. Solution	poor	1	2	3	4	5	outstanding
4. Thought	poor	1	2	3	4	5	outstanding

Comments:

STYLE:

1. Creativity	poor	1	2	3	4	5	outstanding
2. Realism	poor	1	2	3	4	5	outstanding
3. Professionalism	poor	1	2	3	4	5	outstanding
4. Extras	poor	1	2	3	4	5	outstanding

Comments:

OVERALL SCORE: poor 1 2 3 4 5 outstanding

FORM 2

ROLE PLAY EVALUATION: TRAINING (B)

NAME:

DATE:

CLASS:

CONTENT:

1. Preparation	poor	1	2	3	4	5	outstanding
2. Alternatives	poor	1	2	3	4	5	outstanding
3. Solution	poor	1	2	3	4	5	outstanding
4. Thought	poor	1	2	3	4	5	outstanding

Comments:

STYLE:

1. Creativity	poor	1	2	3	4	5	outstanding
2. Realism	poor	1	2	3	4	5	outstanding
3. Professionalism	poor	1	2	3	4	5	outstanding
4. Extras	poor	1	2	3	4	5	outstanding

Comments:

OVERALL SCORE: poor 1 2 3 4 5 outstanding

NOTES AND COMMENTS ON THE TRAINING ROLE PLAYS

Read.

ROLE PLAY 4

Role Conflict

ROLE CONFLICT

Introduction

The set of activities or behaviors expected of any person occupying a certain position is known as a role. Each salesperson occupies a role within an organization. Occupying a role carries certain risks. One of these risks is called role conflict. Role conflict occurs when two or more role partners of the role set have expectations that are incompatible. Role partners for sales representatives include management, customers, suppliers, peers, and family. When role partners' expectations differ, the salesperson experiences role conflict.

Conflict is not always negative. A certain level of conflict keeps the job challenging. There is a point, however, at which the conflict can become damaging to the salesperson's performance and even threaten his or her ability to perform the sales job. At some level of role conflict, performance and job satisfaction will decrease.

Salespeople are susceptible to role conflict because of the nature of their role. The salesperson occupies what is commonly called the boundary position. The salesperson is figuratively the boundary line between customer and corporation. This boundary brings them into frequent conflict between what the customer wants and what the company will allow. The salesperson wants to keep both parties happy. The salesperson is also susceptible to role conflict because of the very large number of role partners that he/she works with. The sheer number of customers, corporate support people, family, and peers guarantee the salesperson that conflict is going to occur.

Role conflict can be even more damaging when the company's demands conflict with family requirements. For example, the company may send the salesperson out of town for business on his/her child's birthday. Resulting conflicts at home will typically have a direct effect on job performance. At a minimum, role conflict will increase stress and lower job performance.

Role conflict can directly affect a sales representative's rewards. For example, if a sales rep consistently sides with the customer breaking some corporate policy, the rep can be officially or unofficially sanctioned (lack of a raise or promotion). If a rep strictly abides by corporate regulations, he or she may lose accounts and thus not make quota or bonus, or fail to be promoted. This is the essence of the role conflict problem. Someone is not going to be entirely happy with the outcome of sales reps' solutions unless they are very innovative or very good at selling their solutions.

This role play examines role conflicts at work and at home. (We recommend that both role plays be combined into one to show home and work conflict). The conflict begins with a typical conflict between an EDD salesperson and a customer. The customer needs a small favor that goes against company policy. The EDD salesperson visits with her manager for guidance but eventually must solve the problem individually (Scenario A). The day only gets worse when the salesperson goes home to her spouse and must inform him that he is going to have to rearrange his schedule because she has been asked by EDD to travel overnight to a business seminar (Scenario B). The second role conflict scenario is designed to show a role conflict between work and family responsibilities and to generate additional classroom discussion.

Role Conflict: Role Play

SCENARIO A

Jennifer King is meeting with Dr. Ron Royal who is the chief physician at Temple Clinic. Dr. Royal has been a steady customer of Jennifer's for the four years that she has been in the Richmond territory. In Scene 1, Jennifer is making a routine sales call on the Temple Clinic and has just been shown in to Dr. Royal's office. Royal tells Jennifer that he has gotten a new directive from the local health department that all of his staff has to be immunized for hepatitis. Since EDD has a well-known hepatitis drug, he wants to place a one-time order for the drug. Jennifer values Royal's business but knows that a company policy will be violated if she places the order directly through LinkPlus. In Scene 2, Jennifer visits with her boss Earl Prince to get approval to violate the policy.

SCENE 1

As Jennifer enters Ron Royal's office, Royal states, "You are just the person I need to see." Jennifer replies, "That's the kind of customer attitude I like to see." Royal continues, "I know this is a little unusual but I need to buy 25 vials of Hydrazene for the clinic staff and I would like you to set up an account for me so I don't have to go through a wholesaler." He then explains to Jennifer about the local health department requirement and how he doesn't want to go through the hassle and expense of buying the product from the wholesaler. Jennifer responds with "I'd like to help, but EDD won't let me open an account for a one-time small purchase because of the administrative expenses." Royal responds, "Jennifer, I've been prescribing your drugs for a long time and I believe in them, but I need this small favor from you." Jennifer says that she will see what she can do and get back to him.

SCENE 2

The second scene is with Jennifer and her boss, Earl Prince. Jennifer explains the situation emphasizing the importance of the account to her and the company and that she needs his signature to approve the direct sale to the new account. Earl states that this policy has come down from above and that he really is not supposed to violate the new account procedure. "I would really like you to solve your problem some other way. Oh, and by the way, I need you to represent the company at the AMA convention on Thursday and Friday. You are the only salesperson who has not had a turn at one of these conventions and I think it will be important experience for you." Jennifer leaves wondering how she is going to solve her dilemma with Dr. Royal.

SCENE 3

The third scene is yours and can be solved in whatever way you wish. The scene can star one, two, or all three characters. You must discuss alternatives in either Scene 2 or 3 before choosing a final solution.

SCENARIO B

Jennifer King has finally ended her day (Monday) at the office and is home with her husband Gary. They begin with the usual chit-chat and small talk. As they talk about their day's activities, Jennifer mentions that Thursday and Friday nights she is going to have to stay in Chicago for business meetings. Gary is not happy that she is going to be out of town again and that he is going to have to take care of little Johnny (age 5). A verbal fight ensues about her career and what it is doing to him and little Johnny.

SCENE 1

The scene begins with Jennifer coming home from work to her husband Gary who also just got home. The two begin some basic small talk and then each begins describing part of their day. Jennifer tells Gary what a terrible day she had. "Everybody seemed to want something from me today. All I did was put out one brush fire after another." Gary responds, "That's nothing, my day was one of those disaster days that you pray will never happen again. I'm looking forward to my poker game Thursday night." Jennifer responds somewhat hesitantly, "Gary, I've got bad news. I've been told to be in Chicago Thursday and Friday for seminars designed for the American Medical Association. Earl said that it's absolutely vital that I'm there to visit with some of my customers." Gary explodes, "Not again! I'm getting sick and tired of you being on the road. This is twice this month. I keep having to change my plans and little Johnny needs his mother. I can't be both mother and father to him." Jennifer angrily responds that this is her career and that they need both incomes to live as they want to live. "You agreed with me taking this job." The scene continues and eventually will fade out.

Characters

1. Salesperson: Jennifer King or Jack Nobel
2. Customer: Ron Royal or Dina Duke
3. Sales manager: Earl Prince or Kathy Knight
4. Spouse: Gary King or Janice Nobel

Character Descriptions

Name: Kathy Knight		
Gender: F	**Age:** 40	**Marital Status:** Married
Education: BA, University of South Carolina		
Title: Sales Manager		**Office Location:** Richmond
Reports To:	District Manager, New York City	
Employment History:	2 years with competitor; 7 years as a manager, 2 years self-employed and 6 years with Pharmiceaux.	
Personality:	Risk-taker; good with young employees; good sense of humor.	
Notes:	Husband is a doctor; turned down a lateral move; likes to travel.	
Grapevine:	Superior evaluations.	

Name: Earl Prince		
Gender: M	**Age:** 45	**Marital Status:** Married
Education: BS, University of Maryland		
Title: Sales Manager		**Office Location:** Richmond
Reports To:	District Manager, New York City	
Employment History:	Been with Pharmiceaux for 20 years; 12 years as a manger.	
Personality:	Conservative; loyal to company, doesn't take risks.	
Notes:	Believes in strictly following company policy; has 2 children, (1 in high school).	
Grapevine:	Not likely to be promoted, happy with his life and company.	

Name: Jennifer King		
Gender: F	**Age:** 26	**Marital Status:** Married
Education: BBA, Northern Illinois		
Title: Sales Rep		**Office Location:** Richmond
Reports To:	Sales Manager, Richmond	
Employment History:	4 years as a sales rep; was hired right out of college.	
Personality:	Perfectionist; has a tendency to stress.	
Notes:	Married for 2 years; has been on the road 3 times in the past 2 months.	
Grapevine:	Going through marital counseling.	

Name: Jack Nobel		
Gender: M	**Age:** 26	**Marital Status:** Married
Education: BBA, University of Ohio		
Title: Sales Rep		**Office Location:** Richmond
Reports To:	Sales Manager, Richmond	
Employment History:	4 years as a sales rep.	
Personality:	Loyal, well-liked at work; father is CEO at an engineering firm.	
Notes:	Married for 2 years; has been on the road 3 times in the past 2 months.	
Grapevine:	Going through marital counseling.	

Name: Ron Royal		
Gender: M	**Age:** 54	**Marital Status:** Married
Education: M.D.		
Title: Chief Physician, Temple Clinic		**Office Location:** Richmond
Employment History:	Has been in practice 25 years.	
Personality:	Caring, patient; good administrator.	
Notes:	Family-oriented; 3 children, 2 in college. Avid golfer; slowing down in his work.	
Grapevine:	Excellent customer.	

Name: Dina Duke		
Gender: F	**Age:** 42	**Marital Status:** Married
Education: M.D.		
Title: Chief Physician, Temple Clinic		**Office Location:** Milwaukee
Employment History:	Physician at Temple Clinic for 5 years. Does a lot of administrative detail work for clinic.	
Personality:	Very intelligent; stickler for detail; organized.	
Notes:	Heavy work load.	
Grapevine:	Excellent customer.	

Name: Gary King			
Gender: M	**Age:** 27		**Marital Status:** Married
Education: BS, University of Illinois			
Title: Sales Manager for a local trucking firm.			**Office Location:** Richmond
Employment History:	Sales rep for 4 years, sales manager for last 2 years.		
Personality:	Fiery personality; doesn't like stress.		
Notes:	Likes to hunt, fish and golf. Likes his job.		
Grapevine:	Not likely to be promoted; wants another child.		

Name: Janice Nobel			
Gender: F	**Age:** 25		**Marital Status:** Married
Education: BA, Ohio University			
Title: Compensation analyst for a local insurance firm.			**Office Location:** Richmond
Employment History:	Secretary for 2 years.		
Personality:	Loves children; environmentalist, devout Catholic.		
Notes:	Been married 2 years; has a 2-year-old daughter.		
Grapevine:	Would like her husband to be home more.		

FORM 1

QUESTIONS FOR ROLE CONFLICT ROLE PLAY

NAME:

DATE:

CLASS SECTION:

QUESTION 1: How can management help reduce role conflict?

QUESTION 2: How much does a salesperson's home life affect the salesperson on the job? In what ways can the conflicts at home manifest themselves in the job?

QUESTION 3: What (if anything) can management do to diminish conflict at home and on the job?

QUESTION 4: What alternatives does Jennifer have in dealing with the problems of her customer versus what the company policy has stated?

Alternative 1:

Consequences:

Alternative 2:

Consequences:

Alternative 3:

Consequences:

Alternative 4:

Consequences:

QUESTION 5: What solution would you have for this scenario? Defend your answer.

FORM 2

ROLE PLAY EVALUATION: ROLE CONFLICT (A)

NAME:

DATE:

CLASS:

CONTENT:

1. Preparation	poor	1	2	3	4	5	outstanding
2. Alternatives	poor	1	2	3	4	5	outstanding
3. Solution	poor	1	2	3	4	5	outstanding
4. Thought	poor	1	2	3	4	5	outstanding

Comments:

STYLE:

1. Creativity	poor	1	2	3	4	5	outstanding
2. Realism	poor	1	2	3	4	5	outstanding
3. Professionalism	poor	1	2	3	4	5	outstanding
4. Extras	poor	1	2	3	4	5	outstanding

Comments:

OVERALL SCORE:	poor	1	2	3	4	5	outstanding

FORM 2

ROLE PLAY EVALUATION: ROLE CONFLICT (B)

NAME:

DATE:

CLASS:

CONTENT:

1. Preparation	poor	1	2	3	4	5	outstanding
2. Alternatives	poor	1	2	3	4	5	outstanding
3. Solution	poor	1	2	3	4	5	outstanding
4. Thought	poor	1	2	3	4	5	outstanding

Comments:

STYLE:

1. Creativity	poor	1	2	3	4	5	outstanding
2. Realism	poor	1	2	3	4	5	outstanding
3. Professionalism	poor	1	2	3	4	5	outstanding
4. Extras	poor	1	2	3	4	5	outstanding

Comments:

OVERALL SCORE: poor 1 2 3 4 5 outstanding

NOTES AND COMMENTS ON THE ROLE CONFLICT ROLE PLAY

ROLE PLAY 5

Ethics

ETHICS

Introduction

Ethical considerations in business are becoming more important than ever. Increased government scrutiny of corporate actions, stricter interpretation of existing laws and development of new, tighter regulations, and more severe penalties for failure to follow ethical business practices are driving firms to formally recognize the importance of ethical business practices. In many industries, such as defense contracting, high ethical standards are important because of past abuses which have led to contractors being declared ineligible for competing on new contracts.

Many firms have formally adopted ethical standards or have even established ethics offices or departments to monitor the ethical practices of the individuals within the firm. Violation of the ethical standards can lead to penalties ranging from unfavorable performance evaluations to termination.

The issue of ethics is particularly important to salespeople and sales managers. Sales managers are responsible for reinforcing the company's ethical standards to its salespeople. Especially for field salespeople, the sales manager's support for ethical standards is important, because the sales manager is often the main contact between the salesperson and the selling firm. Firms need salespeople to uphold high ethical standards because salespeople represent the company to its customers. Unethical practices on the part of a salesperson can color the attitude of the customer toward the selling company as a whole. This can have a lasting impact on the relationship between the customer and the seller. For example, in industries where long-term supply agreements with a limited number of suppliers are becoming the norm (such as the auto industry) it is important that there be a high level of trust between the buyer and the seller. Trust depends on the existence of high ethical standards. If a salesperson acts in an unethical way, and breaches a customer's trust, the seller can lose the customer for an extended period.

From a sales management standpoint, however, monitoring salesperson adherence to ethical standards can be difficult. Salespeople often operate in the field, outside the direct control of a manager. Salespeople paid on a commission basis may argue that meeting tough ethical standards cuts into their compensation. Salespeople may also argue that prevailing industry practices are such that having high ethical standards will put them at a disadvantage with their competitors.

Salespeople are also often placed in situations where it seems that unethical practices are the only way to get or keep an account. This leads to role conflict, as salespeople are caught between opposing forces on ethical standards. This is the situation faced by the salesperson and sales manager in the next role play. The customer has asked the salesperson to act in an unethical fashion and the salesperson, following company policy, has refused. The sales manager, while sympathizing with the salesperson's position, has made it clear that the salesperson must maintain the customer's business. The task for the salesperson is to avoid losing the business while not violating company policy.

NOTE

In the pharmaceutical industry the salesperson will attempt to sell the doctor on the benefits of the drug and will try to close a sale, but orders are not taken as they are in many other industries. The doctor, if sold, will prescribe the drug to appropriate patients. The salesperson is evaluated in part, by management's monitoring of sales by zip code which is provided by an independent sales tracking firm.

Ethics Role Play

SCENARIO

Salesperson Roberta Swenson is talking with Dr. Mel Patterson at a Ulsir EX seminar being sponsored by EDD. The seminar was arranged by Swenson with a noted national scholar speaking on gastrointestinal disorders. Swenson has invited fifteen specialists in the area to the seminar. She is particularly pleased that Dr. Patterson has attended. Swenson has worked hard maintaining Dr. Patterson's business and, in fact, Dr. Patterson has prescribed Ulsir EX regularly for the past three years.

SCENE 1

Swenson approaches Dr. Patterson, greets him warmly and thanks him for attending the seminar. (The discussion should contain the information in the beginning scenario.) Swenson asks Dr. Patterson what he thinks of the speaker. After a positive response, Swenson kiddingly says "I told you that Ulsir EX was the best drug on the market for ulcers. I really have appreciated your business over the past few years and I look forward to more of the same in the future." Dr. Patterson responds by implying that he may be changing drugs for the future. "What?" replies Swenson. "Why?" Dr. Patterson states, "I need a new VCR for my waiting area and the rep for Myopic drugs has promised me one if I would strongly consider his drug. You know it is a pretty good drug." Swenson says that she does not want to lose Patterson's business. "Well, get me my VCR and maybe we can maintain the status quo." Swenson replies that EDD has a strict policy on these type of "gifts." "We can't give these kind of incentives. My boss, Doug Douglas, won't allow it." Patterson responds, "Roberta, you're a bright young woman. You figure it out."

SCENE 2

Swenson has a meeting with her manager, Doug Douglas. Swenson tells Doug that she has a problem and reviews the situation. Doug becomes enraged that a doctor is trying to extort a VCR from EDD. Doug reaches for the phone, "I'm going to call that quack and tell him what I think of his values." Swenson tries to calm Doug by stating that it would guarantee that EDD would lose the business. Swenson explains how important the account is because of the amount of business that Patterson has given her in the past. She tells Douglas, "This account probably is my 4th or 5th most productive account." The two then discuss various alternatives to keep the business and the long-term consequences of each alternative. Finally, Douglas says, "I'll do my best to back you. Roberta, play it smart, but whatever you do, *don't lose the account.*"

SCENE 3

The third scene is yours and can include any of the characters and be in any location. Remember there is no correct answer. Consider the alternatives and consequences and resolve Roberta's dilemma.

Characters

1. Salesperson: George Lymberopolous or Roberta Swenson
2. Customer: Dr. Mel Patterson or Dr. Myra Lolitch
3. Sales Manager: Doug Douglas or Darla Goode

Character Descriptions

Name: Darla Goode		
Gender: F	**Age:** 45	**Marital Status:** Married
Education: BBA, Northeast Louisiana State		
Title: Sales Manager		**Office Location:** Minneapolis
Reports To:	District Manager, Chicago	
Employment History:	Started as sales rep, moved up to training, has been in management for 9 years.	
Personality:	Likeable; stern but fair; easygoing; prefers to avoid controversy.	
Notes:	Sensitive to the policies and rules of the company; has 2 children and 3 dogs.	
Grapevine:	Possible candidate for district manager.	

Name: Doug Douglas		
Gender: M	**Age:** 54	**Marital Status:** Married
Education: BBA, Boise State University		
Title: Sales Manager		**Office Location:** Minneapolis
Reports To:	District Manager, Chicago	
Employment History:	Been with Pharmiceaux for 22 years, 15 years as a manager.	
Personality:	Likeable; stern but fair; prefers to avoid controversy.	
Notes:	4 children (2 in college), loyal to company, has plateaued with Pharmiceaux; avid golfer.	
Grapevine:	Possible early retirement candidate.	

Name: Roberta Swenson		
Gender: F	**Age:** 33	**Marital Status:** Single
Education: BBA, St. Thomas MBA, University of Minnesota		
Title: Senior Sales Rep		**Office Location:** Minneapolis
Reports To:	Sales Manager, Minneapolis/St. Paul	
Employment History:	Been with Pharmiceaux for 6 years.	
Personality:	Motivated; self-starter; leadership qualities; aggressive; straightforward, no-nonsense; follows the rules.	
Notes:	Top performer for 1991; avid skier; likes outdoor activities.	
Grapevine:	May be moving to marketing department.	

Name: George Lymberopolous		
Gender: M	**Age:** 34	**Marital Status:** Single
Education: BBA, James Madison MBA, University of Virginia		
Title: Senior Sales Rep		**Office Location:** Minneapolis
Reports To:	Sales Manager, Minneapolis/St. Paul	
Employment History:	Been with Pharmiceaux for 10 years.	
Personality:	Motivated; goal-oriented; leader; puts company goals ahead of personal goals.	
Notes:	Active in community; avid golfer; consistently in top third in sales.	
Grapevine:	In line for National Accounts position.	

Name: Dr. Mel Patterson		
Gender: M	**Age:** 48	**Marital Status:** Married
Education: MD, State Medical University		
Title: Physician		**Office Location:** Minneapolis
Employment History:	Family Practitioner.	
Personality:	Abrasive; greedy; competent; dedicated.	
Notes:	Is the senior partner in a large practice.	
Grapevine:	Opinion leader in the medical community and will use his influence.	

<table>
<tr><td colspan="2">Name: Dr. Myra Lolitch</td><td colspan="2"></td></tr>
<tr><td colspan="2">Gender: F</td><td>Age: 42</td><td>Marital Status: Married</td></tr>
<tr><td colspan="4">Education: MD, State Medical University</td></tr>
<tr><td colspan="3">Title: Physician</td><td>Office Location: Minneapolis</td></tr>
<tr><td>Employment History:</td><td colspan="3">Family Practitioner</td></tr>
<tr><td>Personality:</td><td colspan="3">Abrasive; greedy; competent; dedicated.</td></tr>
<tr><td>Notes:</td><td colspan="3">Is the senior partner in a large practice.</td></tr>
<tr><td>Grapevine:</td><td colspan="3">Opinion leader in the medical community and will use her influence.</td></tr>
</table>

FORM 1

QUESTIONS FOR ETHICS ROLE PLAY

NAME:

DATE:

CLASS SECTION:

QUESTION 1: Is providing a VCR to a customer in order to receive their business a kickback? Why or why not?

QUESTION 2: What are the long-term consequences of giving the VCR to Dr. Patterson?

QUESTION 3: What is the difference between a kickback and an incentive?

QUESTION 4: What are the realistic alternatives in this case?

Alternative 1:

Consequences:

Alternative 2:

Consequences:

Alternative 3:

Consequences:

Alternative 4:

Consequences:

QUESTION 5: How should Roberta resolve this dilemma?

FORM 2

ROLE PLAY EVALUATION: ETHICS

NAME:

DATE:

CLASS:

CONTENT:

1. Preparation	poor	1	2	3	4	5	outstanding
2. Alternatives	poor	1	2	3	4	5	outstanding
3. Solution	poor	1	2	3	4	5	outstanding
4. Thought	poor	1	2	3	4	5	outstanding

Comments:

STYLE:

1. Creativity	poor	1	2	3	4	5	outstanding
2. Realism	poor	1	2	3	4	5	outstanding
3. Professionalism	poor	1	2	3	4	5	outstanding
4. Extras	poor	1	2	3	4	5	outstanding

Comments:

OVERALL SCORE: poor 1 2 3 4 5 outstanding

NOTES AND COMMENTS ON THE ETHICS ROLE PLAY

ROLE PLAY 6

Purchasing

PURCHASING

Introduction

It is a prerequisite to good business that the seller understand the customer and his/her problems. The seller must conduct a need analysis to determine the real "need" of the customer. This analysis will require multiple sales calls, possibly even before a single order is placed. The rule of thumb is that the seller should do more *listening* than talking. The salesperson must then communicate the customer's needs back to the company. The customer of the '90s has higher expectations of quality and value, and very low tolerance for poor service. Particularly with large customers, salespeople must provide a high level of personalized service to survive in these globally competitive times.

Purchasing agents have also changed. As a whole, they are better educated than the previous generation. Pressure on the purchasing agent has increased to become very "bottom-line" oriented. The sales call of ten years ago typically began with some chit-chat and friendly dialogue. Today, partially because of tough economic times, the sales presentation is more fact-oriented and less concerned with small talk and "how's the family" conversation. This does not minimize the need to build long-term relationships with a buyer. Relationship selling, a concept that is a mainstay in Japanese philosophy, is probably one of the hottest terms in selling. A seller has a responsibility to create a long-term partnership with the customer as a company and the buyer as a person.

The typical sales calls on companies have also changed. Salespeople must often deal with a buying group instead of a single purchasing agent, especially for complex or costly products. Sellers must spend time planning each sales call. Relationships must be established with a variety of people in the organization. There are decision makers and people who have influence on the decision throughout the organization. These people constitute the "buying center." Each member of the buying center should be "sold." It is also important that salespeople recognize that the members of the buying group change over time due to turnover or promotion. Relying on one key person in an organization will eventually cost you. People move, change jobs, change companies, or retire. Relationship selling means building a relationship with companies, not the sole individual.

The other big change that has occurred and is continuing is the advent of females and minorities in sales. This has demanded change in buyers and sellers. Sellers and buyers have become much more "professional" in demeanor and methods. The change has been slow in arriving but the evolution of change is progressing.

This role play examines the concept of relationship selling. The salesperson is calling on one of her favorite buyers, only to find that the buyer is no longer employed by the customer company. The relationship must be rebuilt and the customer resold, a job that may prove to be very difficult.

Purchasing Role Play

SCENARIO

The Southwest Methodist Hospital is one of the largest hospitals in the greater Las Vegas area. Mimi Morgan has called on the hospital for the past four years and has had steady business each year. The only person she has ever dealt with was the buyer, Antonio Vargas. Morgan now finds that Vargas has been replaced because of a change in hospital administration. Antonio had been at the hospital "forever" and was very well liked. Morgan had really enjoyed calling on Vargas and always knew that she would leave with an order. The first scene opens with Mimi calling on Dottie Davis, a purchaser who has replaced Antonio. Dottie is all business and has been ordered by her superiors to cut costs and reorganize the purchasing department. The sales call does not go well. Scene 2 has Morgan talking with her boss Danny Chang about the new management at Southwest.

SCENE 1

Mimi Morgan enters Dottie's office and introduces herself to Dottie. She then asks where Antonio is. Dottie replies, "You haven't done your homework. We're under new management and changes have been made." Morgan replies, "I was aware of the new management team but did not know that Vargas was no longer here. Antonio will be missed. I stopped by to check your inventories and see how the supplies were doing." Dottie responds, "Southwest will not be repurchasing its usual order. Your costs are too high! We are looking at alternative suppliers." Morgan responds, "You have always bought from us and have never had problems with our product. We provide better service than any of our competitors and our product is recognized as the best on the market." Dottie responds, "That may be true, but your prices are the highest on the market, too." The scene fades out.

SCENE 2

Mimi walks into her sales manager's office and asks if he has heard of the changes at Southwest. Danny replies that he has and asks if there are problems. "You better believe it. They have replaced Vargas with some young hotshot. The immediate bottom line seems to be the only concern." Chang replies, "I can't say that I'm surprised. That hospital has always been a little fat. I've heard that they laid off twenty people. Looks like they're getting serious about controlling expenses. How are your relationships with other members of the staff?" Morgan replies reluctantly that she always dealt with Vargas and her current contacts are minimal to nonexistent. Chang then begins a discussion about how to get back into the hospital and how to win back the account. The discussion should look at short-term and long-term strategies to keep the account.

SCENE 3

The third scene will consist of the presentation of the strategy to the Southwest hospital problem. The scene may include one, two, or all three of the characters and the location is up to you. How can Morgan maintain the account and satisfy the needs of the new purchaser?

Characters

1. Salesperson: Mimi Morgan or José Avila
2. Sales Manager: Danny Chang or Cindy Polaski
3. Purchaser: Dottie Davis or Bart Hanson

Character Descriptions

Name: Danny Chang		
Gender: M	**Age:** 42	**Marital Status:** Married
Education: BS, Portland State		
Title: Sales Manager		**Office Location:** Las Vegas
Reports To:	District Manager, Los Angeles	
Employment History:	Manager for 15 years; sales rep for 7 years.	
Personality:	No-nonsense; competitive; driven.	
Notes:	Supportive of his people; good with experienced salespeople—gives them room to make decisions; not as good at mentoring; has 3 children.	
Grapevine:	Dependable.	

Name: Cindy Polaski		
Gender: F	**Age:** 35	**Marital Status:** Divorced
Education: BA, University of Pittsburgh		
Title: Sales Manager		**Office Location:** Las Vegas
Reports To:	District Manager, Los Angeles	
Employment History:	Salesperson for 6 years; human resources for 2 years; sales manager for 4 years.	
Personality:	Enthusiastic; goal-driven; friendly; demands full effort.	
Notes:	The job is her life; wants a district manager position; avid skier.	
Grapevine:	Possible promotion.	

Name: Mimi Morgan		
Gender: F	**Age:** 30	**Marital Status:** Married
Education: BA, New Hampshire		
Title: Sales Rep		**Office Location:** Las Vegas
Reports To:	Sales Manager, Las Vegas	
Employment History:	Been with EDD for 7 years; has had same territory for 4 years.	
Personality:	Friendly; energetic.	
Notes:	Won honors during training program; enjoys her job; has always made quota; avid sailor; no children.	
Grapevine:	A career salesperson; does not want management position.	

Name: José Avila		
Gender: M	**Age:** 31	**Marital Status:** Married
Education: BA, University of New Mexico		
Title: Sales Rep		**Office Location:** Las Vegas
Reports To:	Sales Manager, Las Vegas	
Employment History:	Been with EDD 5 years.	
Personality:	Very friendly; has customers that have become close friends; high producer.	
Notes:	Won the last sales contest; avid golfer; parents are from Mexico.	
Grapevine:	Career sales.	

Name: Bart Hanson		
Gender: M	**Age:** 33	**Marital Status:** Married
Education: BS, University of Wyoming		
Title: Senior Purchaser		
Employment History:	Recent hire at Southwest Methodist; previously Senior Buyer at Kansas City Hospital.	
Personality:	Tough; sensitive; well-organized; all business.	
Notes:	Well-known buyer; an officer in National Purchasers Association; "a tough sell."	
Grapevine:	Hospital still going through changes.	

Name: Dottie Davis		
Gender: F	**Age:** 42	**Marital Status:** Married
Education: BBA, Iowa State		
Title: Senior Purchaser		

Employment History:	Just hired by Southwest Methodist Hospital; previously employed at New York Hospital.
Personality:	No-nonsense, serious; takes no grief from anyone.
Notes:	Hired to cut expenses; tough; gets the job done; bottom-line oriented; skeet shooter.
Grapevine:	Been known to change suppliers to shake things up.

FORM 1

QUESTIONS FOR PURCHASING ROLE PLAY

NAME:

DATE:

CLASS SECTION:

QUESTION 1: How does relationship selling affect the sales process?

QUESTION 2: What mistakes did Mimi make in managing the Southwest Medical Hospital account?

QUESTION 3: What approach should Mimi take to maintain business in the long run?

QUESTION 4: What are the realistic alternatives in this case?

Alternative 1:

Consequences:

Alternative 2:

Consequences:

Alternative 3:

Consequences:

Alternative 4:

Consequences:

QUESTION 5: As a manager, how would you solve this problem?

FORM 2

ROLE PLAY EVALUATION: PURCHASING

NAME:

DATE:

CLASS:

CONTENT:

1. Preparation	poor	1	2	3	4	5	outstanding
2. Alternatives	poor	1	2	3	4	5	outstanding
3. Solution	poor	1	2	3	4	5	outstanding
4. Thought	poor	1	2	3	4	5	outstanding

Comments:

STYLE:

1. Creativity	poor	1	2	3	4	5	outstanding
2. Realism	poor	1	2	3	4	5	outstanding
3. Professionalism	poor	1	2	3	4	5	outstanding
4. Extras	poor	1	2	3	4	5	outstanding

Comments:

OVERALL SCORE: poor 1 2 3 4 5 outstanding

NOTES AND COMMENTS ON THE PURCHASING ROLE PLAY

ROLE PLAY 7

Territories

TERRITORIES

Introduction

Territories are comprised of a number of present and potential customers located in a geographic area. A territory can be assigned to a salesperson, a branch office, or a market intermediary, such as a manufacturer's representative. Territories are established to ensure that the potential market has proper coverage with minimum overlap. Territories are also effective methods of increasing salesforce interest and effectiveness in selling, since each territory is in effect a small profit center.

The design of a territory is based on some form of basic control unit. Typically political boundaries such as states, counties, parishes, cities, zip codes, or metropolitan statistical areas are used. Territories can also be divided by product category or by customer type such as institutions, manufacturers, or retailers. In theory, all territories are supposed to be equal in potential and workload. The key to territory design is the number and size of existing and potential customers, not the geographics. A territory *should* be designed based on purchasing power rather than square miles. Salespeople want to minimize travel and maximize sales potential.

In reality, equivalent sales territories rarely occur. It is difficult to make all territories equal because the firm has to cover all the accounts. For example, a firm might divide Illinois into two territories; Chicago and downstate Illinois. Downstate Illinois would require much higher levels of travel time to reach the same number of customers.

Territory assignments are of critical importance to a salesperson. Some territories are very rewarding and other territories require extensive development. The territory can affect the sales representative's compensation. Bonuses and commissions are directly attached to sales. A strong territory means a better chance at added financial compensation. Disagreements between managers and salespeople can become very heated based on territory assignments or adjustments. Perhaps you begin to see the problems in territory design and management.

This role play explores what happens when a territory, through product innovation, suddenly has more potential than a single salesperson can tap. As frequently occurs in industry, management has decided that the territories need to be reorganized to try and capture the additional potential. The first problem is how to physically redivide a territory(s). Second, how does the manager convince the affected salespeople to agree to the change? Complicating this task is the fact that one of the salespeople involved is a top performer. In this role play, EDD must change a territory that has for several years been very successfully managed by a senior salesperson who has developed extensive customer relationships in the territory. By taking away big accounts and reassigning them to a new salesperson, EDD may indirectly lower the salesperson's compensation.

The sales manager in this role play must redivide the territory, trying to appease the senior salesperson while at the same time creating a new territory that allows a new salesperson a strong chance of success.

Territories Role Play

SCENARIO

Vinnie Canseca has been a sales representative for EDD for the past ten years. Oakland has been his territory for seven of the past ten years. Canseca has been among the top three salespeople in the company for the past five years. He is very well respected by his peers and customers.

Canseca's current territory consists of 120 doctors and three large hospitals. Recently, EDD has acquired Pharmipro from a Japanese research firm and the sales of the product are expected to be substantial. Canseca is looking forward to the new potential. He has never been afraid of a challenge.

Howard Sierra has been Canseca's sales manager for the past four years in the San Francisco district. There are six salespeople who report to him with three located in San Francisco and one (Canseca) in Oakland. Because of the recent addition of Pharmipro, analysis indicates that the Oakland territory has more potential than one rep can handle. Sierra is worried about rearranging Canseca's territory. Canseca is a rather emotional person who prefers to be left alone and just do his job. Even though Canseca frequently trained rookies in the past, he is not thrilled with training new people. The surprising aspect is that Canseca has excellent interpersonal skills with the doctors he calls on and is very well liked, with a number of long-term customers. Canseca is currently training Jamal Washington, a new recruit straight from the University. Sierra plans on using Washington in the new territory if he can figure out how to create it.

SCENE 1

The first scene has Canseca and Sierra meeting. Sierra explains how sales potential has increased throughout the district because of the addition of the new product. He compliments Canseca on his development of the territory and his past success. He then informs Canseca that some restructuring is necessary. Howard says that he is assigning Jamal Washington to part of Canseca's territory. Canseca is very unhappy and expresses his concern about losing customers that he has served for years. "They trust me. They're not going to do business with some beginner. I've worked hard. Don't take my customers away from me!" Sierra replies that he will think about it and do what he can.

SCENE 2

Scene 2 begins with Canseca, Washington, and Sierra all meeting to discuss the division of the new territory. Sierra tells Canseca that he is going to give Washington West Oakland. Canseca angrily replies that West Oakland contains some of his best customers. He has spent the past two years developing the new hospital, which is the largest account in West Oakland. "Give Washington the new accounts and some of my mediocre accounts." Washington responds by saying that he doesn't mind developing new accounts but he needs some sizable accounts to be fairly compensated. Canseca subtly threatens to quit and take his accounts with him if his territory is changed. The scene continues with various alternatives being suggested and discussed, but at least one of the salespeople rejects each plan.

SCENE 3

Scene 3 is yours to resolve the situation. The scene may contain any of the above characters. Be realistic and defend your choice.

Characters

1. Sales Manager: Howard Sierra or Rebecca Goldberg
2. Veteran Salesperson: Vinnie Canseca or Nancy Chee
3. Rookie Salesperson: Jamal Washington or Jennifer Roth

Character Descriptions

Name: Rebecca Goldberg		
Gender: F	**Age:** 34	**Marital Status:** Married
Education: BBA, Lehigh University		
Title: Sales Manager		**Office Location:** San Francisco
Reports To:	District Manager, Los Angeles	
Employment History:	Hired as a manager from competitor.	
Personality:	Sensitive to employees; company profit takes priority; fair; wants to be liked and respected.	
Notes:	District has always been profitable; spends a lot of time "putting out fires"; chess player.	
Grapevine:	Very loyal to the company.	

<table>
<tr><td colspan="3">Name: Howard Sierra</td></tr>
<tr><td>Gender: M</td><td>Age: 37</td><td>Marital Status: Married</td></tr>
<tr><td colspan="3">Education: BA, Murray State University</td></tr>
<tr><td colspan="2">Title: Sales Manager</td><td>Office Location: San Francisco</td></tr>
<tr><td>Reports To:</td><td colspan="2">District Manager, Los Angeles</td></tr>
<tr><td>Employment History:</td><td colspan="2">Salesperson for 4 years; manager for 6 years; previously worked for competitor.</td></tr>
<tr><td>Personality:</td><td colspan="2">Sensitive to employees; company profit takes priority; fair; wants to be liked and respected.</td></tr>
<tr><td>Notes:</td><td colspan="2">District has always been profitable; spends a lot of time "putting out fires"; owns a Harley.</td></tr>
<tr><td>Grapevine:</td><td colspan="2">Very loyal to the company.</td></tr>
</table>

<table>
<tr><td colspan="3">Name: Nancy Chee</td></tr>
<tr><td>Gender: F</td><td>Age: 43</td><td>Marital Status: Widowed</td></tr>
<tr><td colspan="3">Education: BA, Oklahoma State University</td></tr>
<tr><td colspan="2">Title: Senior Sales Rep</td><td>Office Location: Oakland</td></tr>
<tr><td>Reports To:</td><td colspan="2">Sales Manager, San Francisco</td></tr>
<tr><td>Employment History:</td><td colspan="2">10 years with Pharmiceaux; same territory for 7 years.</td></tr>
<tr><td>Personality:</td><td colspan="2">Goal- and task-oriented; very competitive; competent; dependable; very personable.</td></tr>
<tr><td>Notes:</td><td colspan="2">Among the top 3 sales people in Pharmiceaux for last 5 years; needs little supervision; strong customer advocate; Native American advocate.</td></tr>
<tr><td>Grapevine:</td><td colspan="2">Likely to produce for a long time.</td></tr>
</table>

Name: Vinnie Canseca			
Gender: M	**Age:** 43	**Marital Status:** Married	
Education: BS, Ball State University			
Title: Senior Sales Rep		**Office Location:** Oakland	
Reports To:	Sales Manager, San Francisco		
Employment History:	10 years with Pharmiceaux; same territory for 7 years.		
Personality:	Strong customer advocate; among top 5 sales people in Pharmiceaux for last 5 years; needs little supervision; baseball fanatic.		
Notes:	Likely to produce for a long time.		
Grapevine:	Needs work on interpersonal skills.		

Name: Jamal Washington			
Gender: M	**Age:** 22	**Marital Status:** Single	
Education: BBA, Slippery Rock			
Title: Sales Rep		**Office Location:** San Francisco	
Reports To:	Sales Manager, San Francisco		
Employment History:	Recent graduate; just finished training.		
Personality:	Very ambitious; self-assured; eager to succeed.		
Notes:	Student House of Representatives in college; is used to being a leader; model student; likes the nightlife.		
Grapevine:	High potential.		

Name: Jennifer Roth		
Gender: F	**Age:** 22	**Marital Status:** Single
Education: BS, Columbia University		
Title: Sales Rep		**Office Location:** San Francisco
Reports To:	Sales Manager, San Francisco	
Employment History:	Recent graduate; just finished training.	
Personality:	Leader; very ambitious; self-assured; eager to succeed.	
Notes:	President of student organizations; tops in training class; selected Pharmiceaux over other offers because of greatest job potential; women's rights advocate.	
Grapevine:	Potential fast-track candidate.	

FORM 1

QUESTIONS FOR TERRITORIES ROLE PLAY

NAME:

DATE:

CLASS SECTION:

QUESTION 1: How can companies redesign sales territories?

QUESTION 2: What problems occur when territories are redesigned?

QUESTION 3: Is it fair or right to take customers away from Canseca when he is the one who developed the accounts?

QUESTION 4: What alternatives are there for Sierra? How can he keep his people happy and still develop the potential of the region?

Alternative 1:

Consequences:

Alternative 2:

Consequences:

Alternative 3:

Consequences:

Alternative 4:

Consequences:

QUESTION 5: As a manager, how would you solve this territories dilemma?

FORM 2

ROLE PLAY EVALUATION: TERRITORIES

NAME:

DATE:

CLASS:

CONTENT:

1. Preparation	poor	1	2	3	4	5	outstanding
2. Alternatives	poor	1	2	3	4	5	outstanding
3. Solution	poor	1	2	3	4	5	outstanding
4. Thought	poor	1	2	3	4	5	outstanding

Comments:

STYLE:

1. Creativity	poor	1	2	3	4	5	outstanding
2. Realism	poor	1	2	3	4	5	outstanding
3. Professionalism	poor	1	2	3	4	5	outstanding
4. Extras	poor	1	2	3	4	5	outstanding

Comments:

OVERALL SCORE: poor 1 2 3 4 5 outstanding

NOTES AND COMMENTS ON THE TERRITORIES ROLE PLAY

ROLE PLAY 8

Quota

QUOTA

Introduction

Quotas are sales performance goals. The majority of quotas are based on sales volume and are set at a level that is obtainable but that will require the salesperson to push hard to reach quota. Quotas may also be set based on profit or on a level of activity such as prospecting of new accounts. In theory, quotas should be comparable for everyone. In reality, quotas will widely vary because of differences in territory, workload, and salesperson experience.

Management uses quotas to adjust for territory potential, furnish a goal or incentive for the salespeople, control the salespeople's activities, and evaluate productivity. As a result, quotas affect the salesperson in a number of sales decisions such as territory assignment, bonuses for compensation, evaluation, rankings in sales contests, and productivity.

Sales quotas are typically set annually but in some industries can be quarterly or semiannually. The setting of quotas can be controversial. Who sets the quota? There are many approaches in quota setting. Most common is the top-down approach in which top management (i.e., vice president of sales) sets a quota for a region. The regional managers then set quotas for the district. The district managers set quotas for sales managers who then set quotas for their salespeople. Typically, in the top-down approach the salesperson may have little or no input in the quota setting process.

The opposite method is the bottom-up approach which begins with the salesperson having substantial input into the quota. The salesperson meets with the manager and a quota is set. The sales manager takes his/her salespeople's quotas and then has input to the district manager for his/her quota. The process continues up through the channel until the company quotas are set.

There are advantages and disadvantages to each method and many companies will use a combination approach or some other procedure. The quota process is sometimes controversial and is a frequent source of disagreement between the salesperson and management. Since compensation (bonuses, raises) is directly tied to a quota, salespeople have a vested interest in next year's new quota. Salespeople will tell you that at the end of the fiscal year if quota is reached, the quota seems to go up the following year.

This role play begins with a discussion between a sales manager and the district manager about input in setting quotas. The role players will have to discuss advantages and disadvantages of the methods and make a realistic decision as to how the process will occur at EDD.

The second scene will contain a problem with a specific salesperson who has not met quota previously and is not likely to make quota this year. The role players must decide how important meeting quota is and what, if any, sanctions will be levied against the salesperson who is having problems making quota. If EDD is to keep the individual, how can the sales manager get the salesperson back on track?

Quota Role Play

SCENARIO

During a semiannual meeting of EDD's sales management at the headquarters in Fort Worth, Connie Hurkman, sales manager, and Timothy Fagen, the district manager, are informally discussing quotas for the upcoming year. The discussion centers around rumors of quota increases and the resulting problems that will arise within the salesforce. This scene is designed to examine the quota setting process and who should be consulted.

Scene 2 begins with discussion about a particular sales representative (Marvin McCormick) who is in Hurkman's district and seems to be having problems reaching his current quota. McCormick has been with the company for seven years and has had favorable ratings for all but the last and present year. In fact, McCormick has had superior ratings for three of the seven years. McCormick did not meet quota last year, and he is not even close, at this point (January; the fiscal year ends in June), to making quota this year. Policy states that failure to meet quota two years in a row can be reason for termination. Hurkman is fond of McCormick because he was one of her trainers when she entered the job five years ago. She must decide what to do with McCormick because of the quota problems.

SCENE 1

As Hurkman and Fagen are informally talking during a break in the meetings, Hurkman mentions that she has heard that quotas are going up for her salespeople but that quotas were possibly going to be kept the same for other territories. Hurkman continues, "The grapevine even says that the quota raise may be as much as 15 to 20 percent for some of my territories. My people are not going to be happy about these changes." Fagen replies, "They're professionals, they will adapt." Hurkman replies, "Well, yeah, maybe." Hurkman also comments on the upcoming sales contest set to begin in the spring. That contest is based, in part, on group quota results. "This increase in quota is going to put us at a disadvantage." Hurkman strongly argues that she should have been at least consulted about upcoming changes in quota. In fact, she believes that her salespeople should have been consulted about changes and their input should have been incorporated into the proposed changes.

The discussion between these two managers should center on who should make quota assignments and whether top-down, bottom-up or some other quota setting process should be used. The scene should reflect Hurkman's unhappiness about not having input on a decision that affects the performance levels of her people. Fagen listens and then tries to explain why the input was not sought. The last part of this scene can keep quotas as they are or make changes based on the discussion.

SCENE 2

The second scene begins with Fagen asking about McCormick. According to recent reports, he notices that McCormick doesn't have much chance to make quota. Hurkman says "Yeah, I know. I've seen the reports and I'm worried about McCormick. I'm not sure what the problem is. You know McCormick has really performed well in the past. I really think that he is a good salesperson." The district manager replies, "He might have been good once, but quota was not met last year and I strongly doubt it will be met this year. His performance has steadily been going downward. Do something about it or we will have to consider termination." Hurkman says "Let me talk to him first. I think we can solve the problem." Scene ends.

SCENE 3

This scene is between McCormick and Hurkman. The scene focuses on McCormick's current problem with quota. McCormick complains about increasing competition, lack of support, stress and personal problems. Hurkman is sympathetic but emphasizes the seriousness of the situation. "I think you are a good salesperson and I don't want to lose you, but you are in trouble!"

SCENE 4

Scene 4 is yours. It may be a continuation of Scene 3 or it may be an entirely new scene. The characters included are up to you. Provide a solution to the problem. Think about problems that may arise because of your solution. *Be realistic.*

Characters

1. Sales Manager: Connie Hurkman or Nick Cesarone
2. District Manager: Lauren Calle or Timothy Fagen
3. Salesperson: Sally Orlando or Marvin McCormick

Character Descriptions

Name: Lauren Calle		
Gender: F	**Age:** 48	**Marital Status:** Divorced
Education: BBA, UCLA; MBA, University of California, Berekley		
Title: District Manager		**Office Location:** New York

Reports To:	East Regional Manager
Employment History:	Taught at Pepperdine for 2 years. 10 years in management with Fortune 500. Been with Pharmiceaux for 8 years.
Personality:	Straight by the book; believes in management from the top; very friendly.
Notes:	Most knowledgeable about products; photographic memory; 2 children in high school.
Grapevine:	Changes are imminent.

Name: Timothy Fagen		
Gender: M	**Age:** 36	**Marital Status:** Single
Education: BBA, University of Michagan; MBA, Emory		
Title: District Manager		**Office Location:** New York

Reports To:	East Regional Manager
Employment History:	Owned a management consulting firm for 5 years before selling out and coming to work for Pharmiceaux.
Personality:	Authoritative; competitive; frank; energetic.
Notes:	Finished second in the regional manager interview. Wants to be #1. Unforgiving of big mistakes; very fitness-oriented.
Grapevine:	Will shape up a territory or bring in someone new.

Name: Sally Orlando		
Gender: F	**Age:** 35	**Marital Status:** Single
Education: BA, University of North State		
Title: Sales Rep		**Office Location:** Boston
Reports To:	Sales Manager, Boston	
Employment History	Background in marketing and public relations before coming to Pharmiceaux 9 years ago.	
Personality:	Energetic; bubbly; somewhat dramatic.	
Notes:	Made quota for several years; did not make quota last year.	
Grapevine:	Personal problems with long-term boyfriend are interfering with work.	

Name: Marvin McCormick		
Gender: M	**Age:** 38	**Marital Status:** Single
Education: BS, Mid-West Tech		
Title: Sales Rep		**Office Location:** Boston
Reports To:	Sales Manager, Boston	
Employment History:	7 years in advertising sales; been with Pharmiceaux for 10 years.	
Personality:	Energetic; somewhat dramatic.	
Notes:	Sales have been slipping; seems to be moody quite often.	
Grapevine:	Recent death of close family member.	

Name: Connie Hurkman		
Gender: F	**Age:** 32	**Marital Status:** Single
Education: BBA, University of Kansas		
Title: Sales Manager		**Office Location:** Boston

Reports To:	District Manager, New York
Employment History:	Has been with the company for 8 years; previously worked for Baxter.
Personality:	Sentimental; sympathetic; warm; likeable.
Notes:	Occasionally crosses the line between manager and friend—too close to subordinates; open-door policy; her people really like her; loves the outdoors.
Grapevine:	Too trusting; not tough enough at times.

Name: Nick Cesarone		
Gender: M	**Age:** 28	**Marital Status:** Married
Education: BS in Biochemistry, Oregon; MBA, University of Washington		
Title: Sales Manager		**Office Location:** Boston

Reports To:	District Manager, New York
Employment History:	Joined Pharmiceaux immediately after finishing his MBA and has worked his way up from sales.
Personality:	Uptight; workaholic; dominant; competitive.
Notes:	District finished #1 in sales; 1 child, age 2.
Grapevine:	Some of his people think he pushes too hard.

FORM 1

QUESTIONS FOR QUOTA ROLE PLAY

NAME:

DATE:

CLASS SECTION:

QUESTION 1: What is the purpose of a quota system? What advantages does a quota system give management?

QUESTION 2: Who typically determines what quota will be set and why?

QUESTION 3: Should salespeople and first-level sales managers be allowed input into the quota process? What are the arguments for and against their input?

QUESTION 4: What should Hurkman do with Marvin McCormick in the quota scenario? What are Hurkman's realistic alternatives and the consequences of each?

Alternative 1:

Consequences:

Alternative 2:

Consequences:

Alternative 3:

Consequences:

Alternative 4:

Consequences:

QUESTION 5: What solution would you have for this scenario? Defend your answer.

FORM 2

ROLE PLAY EVALUATION: QUOTAS

NAME:

DATE:

CLASS:

CONTENT:

1. Preparation	poor	1	2	3	4	5	outstanding
2. Alternatives	poor	1	2	3	4	5	outstanding
3. Solution	poor	1	2	3	4	5	outstanding
4. Thought	poor	1	2	3	4	5	outstanding

Comments:

STYLE:

1. Creativity	poor	1	2	3	4	5	outstanding
2. Realism	poor	1	2	3	4	5	outstanding
3. Professionalism	poor	1	2	3	4	5	outstanding
4. Extras	poor	1	2	3	4	5	outstanding

Comments:

OVERALL SCORE: poor 1 2 3 4 5 outstanding

NOTES AND COMMENTS ON THE QUOTA ROLE PLAY

ROLE PLAY 9

Leadership

LEADERSHIP

Introduction

Leadership is defined as the use of influence with other people through communication processes to attain specific goals and objectives. Leadership is more than just managing or supervising. Leadership styles differ, but good leaders do share some basic characteristics. A good leader must anticipate problems, not merely react to current crises. The key to anticipation is communication. A leader needs to avoid sending conflicting messages or sending important communications late. Last, the grapevine is a powerful player in the communication game and a good leader needs to be aware of what is being said through the grapevine.

A good leader will use a variety of strategies to influence subordinates to perform in the desired manner. Most strong leaders use selling or persuasion skills to convince others of their point of view. This becomes easier if the leader has created a positive relationship with his or her subordinates. Unfortunately, it occasionally becomes necessary to use negative sanctions when subordinates do not comply with performance standards.

Managers use different leadership approaches. Some managers like to dominate the workplace and will use very tight supervision, rarely involving the salesperson. This type of manager is not leading, although, organizations can be productive under such management. Other managers are afraid to make decisions and do not want "to rock the boat." Clearly, this manager is not leading and the organization will eventually flounder under this style of management. Leaders who are confident in their employees' abilities will allow them room to make decisions, with the manager acting as cheerleader. A good leader will develop personnel who can control themselves and provide structure for those who do not yet have the ability to do so.

Leaders are faced with a variety of problems and opportunities from their personnel. The good leader needs to be a coach (mentor) and deal with personnel problems as they occur. Possibly one of the most difficult aspects of leading is terminating an individual who simply cannot perform to company standards.

In this role play, one role player, acting as an EDD sales manager, will have to deal with four salespeople. Each has a unique problem. The first individual is what is commonly called a "maverick," a salesperson who is very successful in sales but does not play by the rules. Mavericks may lead the organization in sales, but their methods may be questionable and their team play is virtually nonexistent. How does an EDD manager lead this type of individual?

The second problem salesperson is an individual whose sales have slipped and who is rumored to have serious drinking and personal problems. How does an EDD manager deal with problems that occur away from the job yet have a direct effect on the job?

The third individual has not met performance standards for some time. The EDD manager must decide whether he or she can lead the salesperson to being a productive employee or whether the salesperson should be terminated.

The last salesperson is a young sales rep who is lacking confidence. This person is contemplating quitting. The manager sees that with a little more experience, however, the salesperson could be very productive.

All four scenarios call for strong leadership.

Leadership Role Play

SCENARIO

Mary Bartkowski is a first level manager of eight salespeople. She has to manage a variety of difficult personalities. She often thinks to herself, Why me? Why do I get stuck with the pain-in-the-butt types? Mary starts to think about her current "headaches" and begins to wonder what to do with these people. She has four salespeople who follow directions and are at least moderately successful. These are the easy ones. However, the other four present an assortment of problems and personalities.

SCENE 1

Joe Johnson enters Bartkowski's office and demands, "You wanna see me?" Johnson is a top seller and has won a number of selling awards for the company. He is extremely cocky and self-assured. He's good and he knows it. He has been selling for ten years, six for this company.

Bartkowski tells Johnson that his selling performance has been good as usual. Johnson replies, "Good? You mean great, don't you?" Bartkowski says "Yes, but you've missed the last two sales meetings and you never get your reports in on time. I need some cooperation from you." Johnson replies, "I'm a salesman. I sell. I don't have time for this other crap! I bring in a lot of business for this company. I can do it for EDD or I can do it for the competition."

What can Bartkowski do with Johnson? What are her options? Johnson's good and good salespeople are hard to find. How should Bartkowski manage him? Does this affect the other salespeople? Finish the scene with your solution.

SCENE 2

Mary Madison has been selling for EDD for six years. She performed well for the first three or four years. Lately her performance has been down dramatically. There have been complaints from customers about Mary and there are insinuations that she may have a drinking problem. Bartkowski calls Madison into her office to confront her about her poor performance and the rumors. After initial irritated denials, Mary admits that she may be drinking a little more than she should, but she and her husband have been separated for the past six months and he wants a divorce.

What should Bartkowski do? Should personal problems and alcohol/drug problems be treated differently from a managerial problem? What should Bartkowski do with Mary? Finish the scene with your solution.

SCENE 3

Pete Patterson has always been a low performer. He seems to do just enough to get by. He is always below the district average. Bartkowski has about had it with Patterson. She has warned him on several occasions that his performance needs to improve. This morning, she must confront him with evidence that customer satisfaction is low in his territory, and that potential is being missed.

Nothing Bartkowski has done so far has seemed to help. What should Bartkowski do with Patterson? Finish the scene with your solution.

SCENE 4

Kathy Kwan has been with the company less than a year. She just graduated from the University of Hawaii and has completed the standard training. She is still attempting to learn the system. She has good potential and ability but currently is not doing well and is getting discouraged with the job. Management perceives that with a little more experience she can become a good rep. Bartkowski must make sure that Kathy does not quit or let her initial problems affect her future performances.

What should Bartkowski do to manage Kathy? Finish the scene with your solution.

OPTIONAL

This portion of the role play is optional, depending on the requirements of the professor.

Bob Hale has the same job as Mary Bartkowski. Bob is much less tolerant of mistakes and doesn't want anyone challenging his authority or causing him problems. The grapevine on Bob has never been very positive. If you can get the job done, he will reward you; if you have problems, tough! The same scenes can be run, but with a poor leader (Hale) dealing with the four salespeople. The class discussion should focus on the differences in leadership styles between Hale and Bartkowski.

NOTE

The current role play has the sales reps split between Houston and Tulsa. If only one sales manager is used have all salespeople report to the manager in Houston.

Characters

1. Good Leader/Sales Manager: Mary Bartkowski or Don Gibson
2. Poor Leader/Sales Manager: Bob Hale or Patricia Lake
3. Salesperson: Joe Johnson or Lola Andrews
4. Salesperson: Mary Madison or Wayne Ashland
5. Salesperson: Pete Patterson or Suzy Flacker
6. Salesperson: Kathy Kwan or Tyrone Benson

Character Descriptions

Name: Don Gibson		
Gender: M	**Age:** 35	**Marital Status:** Married
Education: BBA, University of Texas at Austin		
Title: Sales Manager		**Office Location:** Houston
Reports To:	District Manager, Dallas	
Employment History:	Has been with the company since graduation; worked as a sales rep for 7 years.	
Personality:	Sensitive to employee needs; puts company goals ahead of personal ones; strong leader.	
Notes:	Youth group leader; active in the community; coaches basketball at area Boy's Club.	
Grapevine:	Being considered for district manager.	

Name: Mary Bartkowski		
Gender: F	**Age:** 34	**Marital Status:** Single
Education: BBA, University of Florida		
Title: Sales Manager		**Office Location:** Houston
Reports To:	District Manager, Dallas	
Employment History:	Started with company right out of school; was sales rep for 7 years, worked her way up.	
Personality:	Success-driven; compassionate; sensitive to subordinates' needs; places company goals ahead of personal ones.	
Notes:	Very active in the community; involved in environmental issues; teaches Sunday School.	
Grapevine:	Being considered for district manager.	

Name: Bob Hale		
Gender: M	**Age:** 33	**Marital Status:** Married
Education: BS, Northern Tech		
Title: Sales Manager		**Office Location:** Tulsa
Reports To:	District Manager, Dallas	
Employment History:	Recruited from competitor; has been with Pharmiceaux for 4 years.	
Personality:	Cocky, chip on his shoulder; confrontational, defensive, negative person; intolerant of mistakes.	
Notes:	He is a loner, always looking out for himself; is resistant to change; passed over for a promotion twice.	
Grapevine:	Future with company is uncertain.	

Name: Patricia Lake		
Gender: F	**Age:** 35	**Marital Status:** Divorced
Education: BA, Southwest Central State University		
Title: Sales Manager		**Office Location:** Tulsa
Reports To:	District Manager, Dallas	
Employment History:	Recruited from the competition; has been with Pharmiceaux for 6 years.	
Personality:	Power hungry, territorial, defensive, confrontational.	
Notes:	Passed over for promotion twice; recently divorced.	
Grapevine:	Future with company is uncertain.	

Name: Tyrone Benson			
Gender: M	**Age:** 22		**Marital Status:** Single
Education: BA, Howard University			
Title: Sales Rep			**Office Location:** Houston
Reports To:	Sales Manager, Houston		
Employment History:	Recent graduate; just finished training.		
Personality:	Lacks maturity; intelligent; outgoing, friendly, likeable.		
Notes:	Class leader, tops in his training class; graduated college with honors, lacks experience. Is having trouble making the adjustment to the industry.		
Grapevine:	High potential; needs a good mentor.		

Name: Kathy Kwan			
Gender: F	**Age:** 22		**Marital Status:** Single
Education: BBA, University of Hawaii			
Title: Sales Rep			**Office Location:** Houston
Reports To:	Sales Manager, Houston		
Employment History:	Recent graduate; just finished training.		
Personality:	Lacks maturity; lacks confidence; intelligent, outgoing; class leader.		
Notes:	Tops in training class, but lacks experience; graduated college with honors.		
Grapevine:	High potential, needs a good mentor.		

Name: Suzy Flacker		
Gender: F	**Age:** 26	**Marital Status:** Single
Education: BBA, Central State University		
Title: Sales Rep		**Office Location:** Houston
Reports To:	Sales Manager, Houston	
Employment History:	2 years with Pharmiceaux; previous experience as department store clerk and telemarketing.	
Personality:	Lacks ambition; no career goals; weak work ethic.	
Grapevine:	Possible termination candidate.	

Name: Pete Patterson		
Gender: M	**Age:** 27	**Marital Status:** Single
Education: BA, South Central Tech		
Title: Sales Rep		**Office Location:** Houston
Reports To:	Sales Manager, Houston	
Employment History:	2 years with Pharmiceaux; previous experience in sales and telemarketing at 2 other companies.	
Personality:	Lacks ambition; class clown—lacks seriousness; is not respected.	
Notes:	Graduated with a 2.2 GPA; weak work ethic; lives on the golf course.	
Grapevine:	Possible termination candidate.	

Name: Joe Johnson		
Gender: M	**Age:** 37	**Marital Status:** Single
Education: Associates Degree, Lake Junior College		
Title: Sales Rep		**Office Location:** Tulsa
Reports To:	Sales Manager, Tulsa	
Employment History:	Been a sales rep with several companies; sold everything from cars to office supplies; been with Pharmiceaux for 6 years.	
Personality:	High ego; cocky, aggressive, demanding, fearless; competitive—borderline unethical.	
Notes:	Has no close friends; respected for his level of sales but not his methods; has been reprimanded on several occasions but has led the district in sales several times.	
Grapevine:	Will never leave sales, but may leave Pharmiceaux.	

Name: Lola Andrews		
Gender: F	**Age:** 38	**Marital Status:** Single
Education: Western State University		
Title: Sales Rep		**Office Location:** Tulsa
Reports To:	Sales Manager, Tulsa	
Employment History:	Sales Rep for 12 years with various companies; with Pharmiceaux for 6 years.	
Personality:	Cocky, confident, aggressive, demanding, competitive.	
Notes:	Plays by the "good-ole-boy" rules; can drink with the best of them.	
Grapevine:	Will never leave sales, but may leave Pharmiceaux.	

Name: Mary Madison		
Gender: F	**Age:** 29	**Marital Status:** Separated
Education: BS, Southwest Tech		
Title: Sales Rep		**Office Location:** Tulsa

Reports To:	Sales Manager, Tulsa
Employment History:	Selling for Pharmiceaux for 6 years.
Personality:	Perfectionist; suffers under high stress; easily discouraged; driven.
Notes:	Recently separated from husband; has had good sales levels; won the top trainee award in her training class.
Grapevine:	Divorce is imminent; rumors of heavy drinking, possibly on the job.

Name: Wayne Ashland		
Gender: M	**Age:** 40	**Marital Status:** Married
Education: BS, Southwest Tech		
Title: Sales Rep		**Office Location:** Tulsa

Reports To:	Sales Manager, Tulsa
Employment History:	Been with Pharmiceaux for 6 years; 10 years of previous selling experience.
Personality:	Good-natured, everybody's friend; very dedicated, ambitious.
Notes:	Steady producer over the years; sales have slipped over the past 2 years; uncertain future; did not reach his dreams.
Grapevine:	Rumors of mid-life crisis and drinking on the job; depressed.

FORM 1

QUESTIONS FOR LEADERSHIP ROLE PLAY

NAME:

DATE:

CLASS SECTION:

QUESTION 1: How can a manager handle a "maverick"? What options do you have with Johnson? Can Bartkowski afford to let Johnson quit?

QUESTION 2: Alcohol and drug problems clearly can affect productivity, but what responsibilities does the company have to an alcoholic? Should an employee be terminated because of alcohol problems? Why or why not?

QUESTION 3: If a manager decides to terminate an employee, what procedures should be followed? If you were the manager, what would you do with Patterson?

QUESTION 4: How can managers lead people who are not producing what is expected of them? Does it matter if the person is a rookie and just lacking confidence?

QUESTION 5: What traits were demonstrated by Bartkowski? How do these traits tie into what you've read/know about leadership?

FORM 2

ROLE PLAY EVALUATION: LEADERSHIP (JOHNSON/ANDREWS)

NAME:

DATE:

CLASS:

CONTENT:

1. Preparation	poor	1	2	3	4	5	outstanding
2. Alternatives	poor	1	2	3	4	5	outstanding
3. Solution	poor	1	2	3	4	5	outstanding
4. Thought	poor	1	2	3	4	5	outstanding

Comments:

STYLE:

1. Creativity	poor	1	2	3	4	5	outstanding
2. Realism	poor	1	2	3	4	5	outstanding
3. Professionalism	poor	1	2	3	4	5	outstanding
4. Extras	poor	1	2	3	4	5	outstanding

Comments:

OVERALL SCORE: poor 1 2 3 4 5 outstanding

FORM 3

ROLE PLAY EVALUATION: LEADERSHIP (MADISON/ASHLAND)

NAME:

DATE:

CLASS:

CONTENT:

1. Preparation	poor	1	2	3	4	5	outstanding
2. Alternatives	poor	1	2	3	4	5	outstanding
3. Solution	poor	1	2	3	4	5	outstanding
4. Thought	poor	1	2	3	4	5	outstanding

Comments:

STYLE:

1. Creativity	poor	1	2	3	4	5	outstanding
2. Realism	poor	1	2	3	4	5	outstanding
3. Professionalism	poor	1	2	3	4	5	outstanding
4. Extras	poor	1	2	3	4	5	outstanding

Comments:

OVERALL SCORE: poor 1 2 3 4 5 outstanding

FORM 4

ROLE PLAY EVALUATION: LEADERSHIP (PATTERSON/FLACKER)

NAME:

DATE:

CLASS:

CONTENT:

1. Preparation	poor	1	2	3	4	5	outstanding
2. Alternatives	poor	1	2	3	4	5	outstanding
3. Solution	poor	1	2	3	4	5	outstanding
4. Thought	poor	1	2	3	4	5	outstanding

Comments:

STYLE:

1. Creativity	poor	1	2	3	4	5	outstanding
2. Realism	poor	1	2	3	4	5	outstanding
3. Professionalism	poor	1	2	3	4	5	outstanding
4. Extras	poor	1	2	3	4	5	outstanding

Comments:

OVERALL SCORE: poor 1 2 3 4 5 outstanding

FORM 5

ROLE PLAY EVALUATION: LEADERSHIP (KWAN/BENSON)

NAME:

DATE:

CLASS:

CONTENT:

1. Preparation	poor	1	2	3	4	5	outstanding
2. Alternatives	poor	1	2	3	4	5	outstanding
3. Solution	poor	1	2	3	4	5	outstanding
4. Thought	poor	1	2	3	4	5	outstanding

Comments:

STYLE:

1. Creativity	poor	1	2	3	4	5	outstanding
2. Realism	poor	1	2	3	4	5	outstanding
3. Professionalism	poor	1	2	3	4	5	outstanding
4. Extras	poor	1	2	3	4	5	outstanding

Comments:

OVERALL SCORE: poor 1 2 3 4 5 outstanding

NOTES AND COMMENTS ON THE LEADERSHIP ROLE PLAY

ROLE PLAY 10

Motivation

MOTIVATION

Introduction

What motivates people? This is a question that has been debated for generations. A variety of things can motivate an individual and what works with one person may not work with the next. People are motivated when they feel a deficiency related to some need. The need (or want) can be more money to buy that new boat or simply more recognition from management. Salespeople can often be motivated by management's recognition that they are doing a good job.

The theories on motivation are numerous and extensive and will not be discussed here (see your Sales Management textbook). However, a good sales manager must be able to motivate salespeople. The first step is knowing what will motivate each person. Some people are self-motivated. There is a strong sense of need for accomplishment, whether it be monetary rewards, career promotions, or feelings of self-worth. The self-motivated salesperson is easy to lead and manage. The job itself is inherently rewarding to the salesperson and performance is typically high.

Motivating the salesperson who is not inherently a self-motivator is much more challenging. The non-self-motivator is motivated by rewards. If rewards are withheld, motivation ceases. Studies have shown that the number one motivator is **money**. Commission salesforces are motivated because no sales means no money. There isn't the comfort of having a salary. The salaried salesperson can still be motivated by money because of raise levels or, more commonly, bonuses based on performance.

Unfortunately, some people may become truly motivated only when a threatened loss of the reward exists. The threat of denying a reward is a form of negative motivation. A manager may indicate to a lackluster salesperson that a lack of dramatic improvement may result in no pay raise or in termination. The motivation occurs because of negative reinforcement.

What motivates a person depends a lot on the person and perhaps the person's career stage. A rookie salesperson might be motivated by the need to succeed. Perhaps the goal is to move into that first management position by age 26. Later, motivation may change to financial security as well as advancement. Toward the end of a career, the motivation may be security, particularly in bad economic times. One long-held theory was that older salespeople cease to be motivated by money. However, some recent evidence tends to argue that for many, money remains the number one motivator throughout the career.

The managers in this role play must decide what to do with a valued salesperson who has been a part of the company for 25 years, but is not performing to expectations. How can they motivate this senior sales rep and, if they cannot, what should they do with the salesperson?

Motivation Role Play

SCENARIO

Gerry Tall has been with EDD for 25 years. He is well respected by the junior sales reps and is well known and liked throughout the company. Gerry has, over the years, developed a clientele based on friendship. Many of these customers have never been called on by any EDD salesperson except Gerry. Gerry has been an excellent salesperson, winning the top sales award seven times, although not in the last six years. Management has noted that Gerry's sales have slipped in the last two years and the number of new customers that Gerry has brought in has been virtually zero. More importantly, new market analysis has shown that Gerry's territory has some untapped potential. While it is not enough to justify creating a new territory, it is disturbing to management that Gerry is making no effort to get this business. Gerry, who is 57, is making about $70,000/year and is financially secure.

SCENE 1

The first scene features Lyle Greenlee (Gerry's immediate boss) and LaDonna Mobley (the district manager) discussing the problem of Gerry. The first scene should lay out the basic facts of the case. The two managers should discuss a variety of possible alternatives, commenting on the negative consequences of each alternative. The first scene will end with Lyle stating that he will have a talk with Gerry.

SCENE 2

Scene 2 opens with Gerry entering Lyle's office. After some basic small talk, Lyle comments that Gerry's performance has slipped in the last couple of years. Gerry responds that he admittedly is not as gung-ho as he used to be, but he still outperforms most of the sales reps in the company. "I've been around 25 years and I've brought this company a lot of business. I think I have the right to slow down some." Lyle responds that there is a lot of potential that is not being developed. "EDD certainly appreciates all of the hard work that you've done for us, and we anticipate that you can continue to help us. However, we need this new business."

SCENE 3

Scene 3 is yours. The scene can continue from Scene 2 or can be a completely new scene. You need to provide a workable solution to the problem. How are you successfully going to motivate Gerry? The scene may feature any of the characters in any location.

Characters

1. Sales Manager: Lyle Greenlee or Andrea Schmidt
2. District Manager: Manuel de la Guardia or LaDonna Mobley
3. Salesperson: Gerry Tall or Elle Durley

Character Descriptions

<table>
<tr><td colspan="3">Name: Manuel de la Guardia</td></tr>
<tr><td>Gender: M</td><td>Age: 35</td><td>Marital Status: Married</td></tr>
<tr><td colspan="3">Education: BBA, University of Puerto Rico</td></tr>
<tr><td colspan="2">Title: District Manager</td><td>Office Location: Los Angeles</td></tr>
<tr><td>Reports To:</td><td colspan="2">West Regional Manager</td></tr>
<tr><td>Employment History:</td><td colspan="2">Rapid promotions; started with the company at age 18 and has worked his way up.</td></tr>
<tr><td>Personality:</td><td colspan="2">Very demanding, aggressive, and autocratic; expects perfection.</td></tr>
<tr><td>Notes:</td><td colspan="2">Youngest district manager in the last 10 years; his district has the highest profit level. Handball expert.</td></tr>
<tr><td>Grapevine:</td><td colspan="2">Probably a future VP.</td></tr>
</table>

Name: LaDonna Mobley			
Gender: F	**Age:** 42		**Marital Status:** Married
Education: BBA, Univ. of Massachusetts; MBA, Dartmouth.			
Title: District Manager			**Office Location:** Los Angeles
Reports To:	West Regional Manager		
Employment History:	Recruited from a major computer company where she was a National Accounts salesperson. Sales manager with Pharmiceaux for 5 years; district manager for 2 years.		
Personality:	Tough, demanding, extremely competitive, very ambitious, fair.		
Notes:	Wants her district to be on top. Recently terminated a 10-year veteran for poor performance. Has season tickets to the opera.		
Grapevine:	Wants a VP job, and maybe not with Pharmiceaux.		

Name: Andrea Schmidt			
Gender: F	**Age:** 26		**Marital Status:** Single
Education: BBA, Arizona State University			
Title: Sales Manager			**Office Location:** Phoenix
Reports To:	District Manager, Los Angeles		
Employment History:	Sales manager for 6 months; previously a sales rep for East Region.		
Personality:	Aggressive, driven, good communication, highly professional.		
Notes:	Inexperienced in management; high performer as a sales rep. Youngest sales manager in company. Fitness fanatic.		
Grapevine:	Being watched closely by management because of youth.		

<table>
<tr><td colspan="3">Name: Lyle Greenlee</td></tr>
<tr><td>Gender: M</td><td>Age: 28</td><td>Marital Status: Single</td></tr>
<tr><td colspan="3">Education: BS, Memphis State</td></tr>
<tr><td colspan="2">Title: Sales Manager</td><td>Office Location: Phoenix</td></tr>
<tr><td>Reports To:</td><td colspan="2">District Manager, Los Angeles</td></tr>
<tr><td>Employment History:</td><td colspan="2">Sales manager for 1 year; previously a sales rep for South Region.</td></tr>
<tr><td>Personality:</td><td colspan="2">Aggressive, driven, good communication, highly professional.</td></tr>
<tr><td>Notes:</td><td colspan="2">Athletic; inexperienced in management; received a good annual review after first year as a manager.</td></tr>
<tr><td>Grapevine:</td><td colspan="2">Fast-tracker.</td></tr>
</table>

<table>
<tr><td colspan="3">Name: Elle Durley</td></tr>
<tr><td>Gender: F</td><td>Age: 57</td><td>Marital Status: Widowed</td></tr>
<tr><td colspan="3">Education: Associates Degree, Community Junior College</td></tr>
<tr><td colspan="2">Title: Senior Sales Rep</td><td>Office Location: Phoenix</td></tr>
<tr><td>Reports To:</td><td colspan="2">Sales Manager, Phoenix</td></tr>
<tr><td>Employment History:</td><td colspan="2">25 years with Pharmiceaux.</td></tr>
<tr><td>Personality:</td><td colspan="2">Well-liked and respected within the company; loyal, easygoing.</td></tr>
<tr><td>Notes:</td><td colspan="2">Brings donuts and cookies to the office every day. Considers the company to be her family since her husband died.</td></tr>
<tr><td>Grapevine:</td><td colspan="2">Content with her current position.</td></tr>
</table>

Name: Gerry Tall		
Gender: M	Age: 56	Marital Status: Married
Education: Associates Degree, County Community College		
Title: Senior Sales Rep		Office Location: Phoenix

Reports To:	Sales Manager, Phoenix
Employment History:	25 years with Pharmiceaux.
Personality:	Easygoing, everybody's friend; loyal to the company.
Notes:	Mentor for younger sales reps; hosts a backyard barbecue each spring.
Grapevine:	Content with current position.

FORM 1

QUESTIONS FOR MOTIVATION ROLE PLAY

NAME:

DATE:

CLASS SECTION:

QUESTION 1: Does Gerry have the right to slow down because of his age and years of service to EDD? Should we expect the same level of sales from him that we do from a 25-year-old?

QUESTION 2: What are some ways that management can motivate salespeople?

QUESTION 3: If Gerry is not able to perform to the levels that management expects, what could be done with him?

QUESTION 4: What are some alternatives available in managing and motivating Gerry? What long-term consequences would occur with each alternative?

Alternative 1:

Consequences:

Alternative 2:

Consequences:

Alternative 3:

Consequences:

Alternative 4:

Consequences:

QUESTION 5: What solution would you have for this scenario? Defend your answer.

FORM 2

ROLE PLAY EVALUATION: MOTIVATION

NAME:

DATE:

CLASS:

CONTENT:

1. Preparation	poor	1	2	3	4	5	outstanding
2. Alternatives	poor	1	2	3	4	5	outstanding
3. Solution	poor	1	2	3	4	5	outstanding
4. Thought	poor	1	2	3	4	5	outstanding

Comments:

STYLE:

1. Creativity	poor	1	2	3	4	5	outstanding
2. Realism	poor	1	2	3	4	5	outstanding
3. Professionalism	poor	1	2	3	4	5	outstanding
4. Extras	poor	1	2	3	4	5	outstanding

Comments:

OVERALL SCORE: poor 1 2 3 4 5 outstanding

NOTES AND COMMENTS ON THE MOTIVATION ROLE PLAY

ROLE PLAY 11

Compensation

COMPENSATION

Introduction

Most new sales representatives initially perceive that compensation means money. In reality, compensation can be financial or nonfinancial. Compensation is really based on reward management. Rewards are used to direct salesperson behavior to attain the objectives of the organization. Financial compensation is comprised of current spendable income and deferred income or benefits.

Current spendable income includes salary, commissions, and bonuses. Companies will typically pay straight salary, straight commission, salary and commission, or salary and bonus. Straight salary or salary and bonus are very useful for industries that have sales jobs including: missionary sales (such as a pharmaceutical company), sales support, seasonal sales, high technology sales, and route sales. From a management standpoint, the advantage of salaried personnel is the level of control over the salesforce and the predictability of total selling expense. Salaried personnel also tend to be more company loyal. The primary disadvantage is the lack of heavy financial incentives to increase sales.

Commission sales personnel are hard to control because their income is directly linked to sales. Commission sales personnel tend to resist activities that are not directly selling-oriented. As a result, paperwork, new customer development, and meetings are often avoided. Commission sales personnel tend to change jobs more frequently than salaried personnel and, as a result, are viewed by management as having little loyalty.

Financial compensation might also include other dimensions such as expense accounts, a company car or car expense, profit sharing, benefits, and stock options. Another form of compensation in many companies is sales contests in which sales representatives can win cash, trips, or merchandise.

Nonfinancial compensation is also a way to reward sales personnel. The range of nonfinancial compensation is as wide as that of financial compensation. Most companies have some form of recognition program in which winners receive accolades, titles, time off, and possibly merchandise or cash. These recognition programs are a very effective way to motivate and compensate many salespeople. Another primary form of nonfinancial compensation is promotions. The problem with promotion is that there are a limited number of positions in sales management and many qualified sales representatives who would welcome a promotion. For every person who is promoted, there are several disappointed yet very qualified people who are not.

Another important nonfinancial form of compensation can simply be referred to as "perks." Perks are status symbols that people can earn. For example, if a company gives cars to its salespeople, the company may offer an upgrade if a salesperson reaches a certain level of performance. The location of office, type of furniture, parking place, and similar niceties can also serve as compensation tools. Last, some companies will pay for personal growth such as a college degree or seminars designed to further educate the salesperson.

This role play begins with a last round interview with a promising applicant who will soon be graduating from college. The offer is made to the recruit and the discussion turns to compensation. The second scene revolves around compensation problems within the company and resulting turnover problems. The role players will need to examine potential effective compensation alternatives.

Compensation Role Play

SCENARIO

Juan Garcia is in the final round of interviews with EDD and has been asked to come to the home office in Fort Worth. Juan is an extremely impressive individual and EDD had him ranked as the top graduate from Duke. He is currently in the office of Sarah Fall, the West Regional Manager, talking about the job. Fall has made an offer to Juan and they begin talking about compensation. Juan tells Fall that he has another offer and that it has a higher starting salary. Fall attempts to persuade Juan by selling him on the entire compensation of the job and the value of working for EDD.

In the second scene, Fall is meeting with Luis Andrade, the vice president of marketing for EDD, and tells him how they just lost signing Garcia. She also mentions that two more top salespeople have recently quit EDD to take similar positions with competitors. Fall and Andrade discuss the current compensation package and begin brainstorming about what can be done to improve morale and the compensation package. The second scene will end with Andrade telling Fall to put a task force together and solve the problem.

SCENE 1

Scene 1 opens with Juan Garcia in the end of an interview with Sarah Fall. Fall tells Juan how impressed the company is with him and that she believes Juan would make a nice addition to EDD. Fall offers him a job and then describes the compensation package. As she finishes, Juan expresses his appreciation but raises a problem with starting salary. "Pharmiceaux is a great company and I think there is a lot of opportunity here but Acme Pharmaceutical has made me an offer with $3,000 more in starting salary." Fall tells Juan that she cannot get him more pay. "Frankly, Juan, I have offered you the top salary that we can offer. The vast majority of our new people begin at $1,500 less than we offered you." Juan responds, "I appreciate your confidence in me. I need a few days to think about the offer." The scene closes with the two shaking hands.

SCENE 2

Fall is in a meeting with Andrade. The scene begins with some small talk and Fall tells Andrade, "We lost Garcia. I really think he is making a mistake. Acme beat us on starting salary, but in the long run I really think he would have done much better with us." Andrade replies, "We lost this one, but I think we have a very competitive starting package. We'll win the next one. I am more concerned about the fact that we just had two more of our salespeople quit and go with a competitor. We need to do something to perk up our morale and improve our compensation." The scene continues with the two of them discussing possible realistic changes including an ongoing contest. The scene will end with Andrade telling Fall to put a task force together and examine the compensation issue and get back to him. "Do it soon. I don't want to lose anybody else."

SCENE 3

The third scene is Fall's solution and will be a report back to Andrade with some detail of what she suggests EDD do to improve the morale and the compensation of the salesforce.

Characters

1. Vice President of Sales: Luis Andrade or Lois McKinney
2. West Regional Manager: Ty Nakamora or Sarah Fall
3. Recruit: Juan Garcia or Jill Benedict

Character Descriptions

<table>
<tr><td colspan="4">Name: Ty Nakamora</td></tr>
<tr><td colspan="2">Gender: M</td><td>Age: 48</td><td>Marital Status: Married</td></tr>
<tr><td colspan="4">Education: BBA, University of San Diego</td></tr>
<tr><td colspan="3">Title: West Regional Manager</td><td>Office Location: Los Angeles</td></tr>
<tr><td>Reports To:</td><td colspan="3">VP of Sales</td></tr>
<tr><td>Employment History:</td><td colspan="3">Been with Pharmiceaux for 8 years; 3 years as a regional manager; hired from a Japanese R&D company</td></tr>
<tr><td>Personality:</td><td colspan="3">Very professional; fair, but tough.</td></tr>
<tr><td>Notes:</td><td colspan="3">Excellent experience. 4 children.</td></tr>
<tr><td>Grapevine:</td><td colspan="3">Seeking a CEO job, possibly with another firm.</td></tr>
</table>

Name: Sarah Fall		
Gender: F	**Age:** 50	**Marital Status:** Married
Education: BBA, Texas Wesleyan University; MBA, Texas Christian University		
Title: West Regional Manager		**Office Location:** Los Angeles
Reports To:	VP of Sales	
Employment History:	Began with Pharmiceaux in Dallas after 3 years in non-profit industry. Has worked her way through the system.	
Personality:	Likeable; hard worker; mentors junior personnel, volunteers for a number of charities.	
Notes:	Has been a "favored" employee because of dedication to the company.	
Grapevine:	In line for promotion to VP of Sales.	

Name: Juan Garcia		
Gender: F	**Age:** 25	**Marital Status:** Single
Education: BBA, NC State; MBA, Duke		
Title: Recruit		
Employment History:	No full-time work experience.	
Personality:	Ego-oriented, ambitious, intelligent, career-oriented. Big tennis player.	
Notes:	#1 in class, impressive resume, numerous honors, graduated with undergrad degree in three years; 2 years experience.	
Grapevine:	Multiple offers; top management potential.	

Name: Jill Benedict			
Gender: F	**Age:** 26	**Marital Status:** Divorced	
Education: BA, Furman; MBA, Georgia Tech			
Title: Recruit			
Employment History:	No full-time work experience.		
Personality:	Very professional, career-oriented, intelligent.		
Notes:	Finished second in class; MBA fully funded; recommendations are impressive; strong analytical skills.		
Grapevine:	Multiple offers, top management potential.		

Name: Luis Andrade			
Gender: M	**Age:** 52	**Marital Status:** Married	
Education: BBA, Texas Christian University; MBA, Texas Christian University			
Title: VP, Sales		**Office Location:** Fort Worth	
Reports To:	Henry Shannon, CEO		
Employment History:	Sales and middle management in food industry; hired as a regional manager for Pharmiceaux, promoted to VP 3 years ago.		
Personality:	Goal- and detail-oriented. Solid leader, visionary.		
Notes:	Has made sweeping changes in organization, but well-liked. Rewards hard work. Avid golfer. 4 children.		
Grapevine:	CEO pleased with his work.		

Name: Lois McKinney		
Gender: F	**Age:** 53	**Marital Status:** Divorced
Education: BA, Boston College; MBA , Dartmouth		
Title: VP, Sales		**Office Location:** Fort Worth
Reports To:	Henry Shannon, CEO	
Employment History:	Sales in the computer industry; middle management at a pharmaceutical competitor. Hired as a regional manager; promoted to VP 5 years ago.	
Personality:	Detail-oriented, workaholic, perfectionist.	
Notes:	Loves to travel when she has time; 5 grandchildren; gourmet chef.	
Grapevine:	CEO material if she can wait for Shannon to retire.	

FORM 1

QUESTIONS FOR COMPENSATION ROLE PLAY

NAME:

DATE:

CLASS SECTION:

QUESTION 1: What should a potential new recruit look for in a compensation package?

QUESTION 2: What are the advantages and disadvantages of running a sales contest? What problems must be overcome to run a successful contest?

QUESTION 3: What conditions might determine whether a company is to use straight commission versus straight salary?

QUESTION 4: What realistic alternatives does the company have for changing the compensation package without dramatically changing the profit structure?

Alternative 1:

Consequences:

Alternative 2:

Consequences:

Alternative 3:

Consequences:

Alternative 4:

Consequences:

QUESTION 5: How would you solve this compensation dilemma for Andrade and what would you include in your report if you were Fall?

FORM 2

ROLE PLAY EVALUATION: COMPENSATION

NAME:

DATE:

CLASS:

CONTENT:

1. Preparation	poor	1	2	3	4	5	outstanding
2. Alternatives	poor	1	2	3	4	5	outstanding
3. Solution	poor	1	2	3	4	5	outstanding
4. Thought	poor	1	2	3	4	5	outstanding

Comments:

STYLE:

1. Creativity	poor	1	2	3	4	5	outstanding
2. Realism	poor	1	2	3	4	5	outstanding
3. Professionalism	poor	1	2	3	4	5	outstanding
4. Extras	poor	1	2	3	4	5	outstanding

Comments:

OVERALL SCORE: poor 1 2 3 4 5 outstanding

NOTES AND COMMENTS ON THE COMPENSATION ROLE PLAY

PART IV

EXECUTIVE PROFILES AND EXTRA CHARACTERS

Name: Gino Ventrella		
Gender: M	**Age:** 45	**Marital Status:** Married
Education: BA, Baylor		
Title: Sales Rep		**Office Location:** Houston
Reports To:	Sales Manager, Houston	
Employment History:	Been with company since college graduation.	
Personality:	Devoted, good mentor, easygoing, sympathetic.	
Notes:	"Married to the company," career sales, 3 kids, coaches little league.	
Grapevine:	Has enough Pharmiceaux stock to retire early.	

Name: Caitlin O'Neil		
Gender: F	**Age:** 33	**Marital Status:** Single
Education: BBA, Fordham University		
Title: District Manager		**Office Location:** Dallas
Reports To:	West Regional Manager	
Employment History:	Hired 3 months ago.	
Personality:	Personable, hard-working and confident, opinionated, animated.	
Notes:	Founder's niece—must prove herself; a leader in college; seems to have her priorities in order.	
Grapevine:	Eventually wants a staff job to learn the business.	

Name: Barry Niekro		
Gender: F	**Age:** 45	**Marital Status:** Divorced
Education: University of Missouri		
Title: District Manager		**Office Location:** Dallas
Reports To:	West Regional Manager	
Employment History:	12 years with a communications company; 12 years with Pharmiceaux in sales.	
Personality:	Clever, impulsive, low-key, "maverick."	
Notes:	Probably will not go any higher in company; excellent salesperson—still noted for sales ability. Bored with management.	
Grapevine:	May return to sales position.	

Name: Cecil Porter		
Gender: M	**Age:** 43	**Marital Status:** Married
Education: BA, Grambling		
Title: Senior Sales Rep		**Office Location:** Baton Rouge
Reports To:	Sales Manager, New Orleans	
Employment History:	Entire career with Pharmiceaux.	
Personality:	Determined, never gives up; likeable, charming.	
Notes:	First African American in Pharmiceaux salesforce 20 years ago. Well-respected, mentor—especially to minorities. Avid fisherman; 3 children.	
Grapevine:	A management favorite.	

Name: Darren Chambliss		
Gender: M	**Age:** 42	**Marital Status:** Married
Education: BA, Vanderbilt		
Title: National Accounts		**Office Location:** Fort Worth
Reports To:	West Regional Manager	
Employment History:	10 years as an independent sales rep; 10 years with Pharmiceaux, last 3 years in National Accounts.	
Personality:	Comfortable with people; handles stress well.	
Notes:	Has performed well throughout career; avid skier; one child.	
Grapevine:	Management is very pleased with his work.	

Name: Jinger Hamm		
Gender: F	**Age:** 38	**Marital Status:** Divorced
Education: BA, University of Wisconsin, Eau Claire		
Title: District Manager		**Office Location:** Seattle
Reports To:	West Regional Manager	
Employment History:	4 years in a chemical firm; 6 years in Pharmiceaux sales, 2 years leadership staff, 4 years National Accounts, recent promotion to District Manager.	
Personality:	Somber, detail-oriented, persevering, self-controlled.	
Notes:	Excellent experience and sales skills; didn't like desk job; 1 child; marathoner.	
Grapevine:	Fast-tracker.	

Name: Gino Key		
Gender: M	**Age:** 60	**Marital Status:** Married
Education: BA, University of Alabama		
Title: Senior Sales Rep and Trainer		**Office Location:** Tampa
Reports To:	Sales Manager, Atlanta	
Employment History:	10 years in chemical industry; 6 years in business, 22 years with Pharmiceaux.	
Personality:	Loves to work, good mentor, considerate, well-liked.	
Notes:	Grandfather; loves to fly; fisherman.	
Grapevine:	2 more years to retirement.	

Name: Shelly Charbaneaux		
Gender: F	**Age:** 25	**Marital Status:** Engaged
Education: BS, Hardin-Simmons		
Title: District Manager		**Office Location:** New Orleans
Reports To:	East Regional Manager	
Employment History:	Been with Pharmiceaux 3 years.	
Personality:	Fair-minded, sentimental, warm.	
Notes:	Good annual reviews; very active in the church.	
Grapevine:	May leave company when she marries.	

Name: Max Groom		
Gender: M	**Age:** 28	**Marital Status:** Divorced
Education: BS, Tech State		
Title: Sales Rep		**Office Location:** Baton Rouge
Reports To:	District Manager, New Orleans	
Employment History:	Been with company for 4 years.	
Personality:	Defensive, sarcastic, impulsive, rebellious.	
Notes:	Reviews have been poor; doesn't get along with his boss; would live on the golf course if he could.	
Grapevine:	In danger of termination.	

Name: Byron Simpson		
Gender: M	**Age:** 40	**Marital Status:** Married
Education: BA, McGill; MBA, University of Western Ontario		
Title: District Manager		**Office Location:** New Orleans
Reports To:	East Regional Manager	
Employment History:	Began with Pharmiceaux at 24, manager at 29.	
Personality:	Warm, sympathetic, sincere, friendly.	
Notes:	2 of his recent salespeople are now sales managers; championship pistol shooter, home defense expert.	
Grapevine:	Good mentor and trainer.	

Name: Howard Taylor		
Gender: M	**Age:** 55	**Marital Status:** Married
Education: BS, Ohio State; MBA, Wharton		
Title: East Regional Manager		**Office Location:** Boston
Reports To:	VP, Sales	
Employment History:	Been with Pharmiceaux for 22 years; product manager for 12 years; previously a chemical engineer for 12 years with a chemical company.	
Personality:	Workaholic, dedicated, intelligent.	
Notes:	Wants a diversity of Pharmiceaux experience.	
Grapevine:	Possible candidate for next VP of Marketing.	

Name: Karen White		
Gender: F	**Age:** 24	**Marital Status:** Single
Education: BA, University of West Virginia		
Title: Sales Rep		**Office Location:** Richmond
Reports To:	Sales Manager, Richmond	
Employment History:	2 years with Pharmiceaux.	
Personality:	Personable; born to sell; problem-solver.	
Notes:	Active in the community; sorority officer, part-time salesperson in college.	
Grapevine:	Career sales, but leaving Pharmiceaux.	

Name: Maria Hernandez		
Gender: F	**Age:** 45	**Marital Status:** Divorced
Education: Lic., University of Guadalajara; MBA, Texas A&M		
Title: Sales Manager, East Regional		**Office Location:** Omaha

Reports To:	District Manager, Denver
Employment History	Sales with 3 companies; began with Pharmiceaux at 30, moved up to sales manager at 38.
Personality:	Vivacious, very well-liked by peers and the office.
Notes:	Career-oriented, mentor; first one into the office each morning.
Grapevine:	May transfer to International Division.

Name: Yolanda Smith		
Gender: F	**Age:** 43	**Marital Status:** Divorced
Education: BBA, Georgia State		
Title: District Manager		**Office Location:** Atlanta

Reports To:	East Regional Manager
Employment History:	Worked her way through school; began with Pharmiceaux at 24.
Personality:	Detail-oriented, motivated, confident.
Notes:	Working on a law degree part-time; 1 year to go.
Grapevine:	May move to legal when degree is completed.

Name: Ron Bradley		
Gender: M	**Age:** 44	**Marital Status:** Married
Education: BBA, Florida State		
Title: District Manager		**Office Location:** Atlanta
Reports To:	East Regional Manager	
Employment History:	Worked at a chemical company, hired at Pharmiceaux as a sales manager, promoted to district manager at 40.	
Personality:	Family-oriented; works hard, plays hard.	
Notes:	Loves water activities, fanatical baseball fan, 3 kids.	
Grapevine:	Does not want to leave Atlanta.	

Name: Luke Jefferson		
Gender: M	**Age:** 52	**Marital Status:** Divorced
Education: BS, Cal State, Pomona		
Title: District Manager		**Office Location:** Seattle
Reports To:	West Regional Manager	
Employment History:	Chemist for 8 years, then moved to sales. Hired by Pharmiceaux at 33, promoted to sales manager at 35, district manager at 45.	
Personality:	Reserved, very efficient, extremely knowledgeable.	
Notes:	Single for the past 10 years; 1 son hired by Pharmiceaux Eastern Region; history buff.	
Grapevine:	Wants a promotion; may move to upper management in production.	

Name: Gary Payton		
Gender: M	**Age:** 48	**Marital Status:** Married
Education: BBA, Colorado State		
Title: District Manager		**Office Location:** Denver
Reports To:	West Regional Manager	
Employment History:	Hired directly out of college; steadily moved up the company ladder.	
Personality:	Athletic, very outgoing, competitive.	
Notes:	Star football player in college, president of the Alumni Association; 2 children.	
Grapevine:	Fast-tracker.	

Name: Shondra Washington		
Gender: F	**Age:** 51	**Marital Status:** Married
Education: BA, University of Denver; MBA, Nebraska (Lincoln)		
Title: District Manager		**Office Location:** Denver
Reports To:	West Regional Manager	
Employment History:	Hired by a large consumer company, obtained MBA, and was promoted to management; hired by Pharmiceaux as district manager.	
Personality:	Detail-oriented, patient, good listener, well-organized.	
Notes:	Skier; husband works for a competitor; 4 children.	
Grapevine:	Possible problems at home.	

Name: Henry Shannon			
Gender: M	**Age:** 60		**Marital Status:** Married
Education: BBA, University of Kentucky; MBA, Tennessee; PhD, University of Chicago			
Title: CEO			**Office Location:** Fort Worth
Reports To:	Board of Trustees		
Employment History:	Sales with a chemical company, rapidly promoted; hired by Pharmiceaux at 42, multiple jobs held.		
Personality:	Gregarious, respected, detail-oriented, competitive.		
Notes:	Chef; photographic memory; 3 children, 5 grandchildren; frequent public speaker.		
Grapevine:	Not leaving any time soon.		

Name: Monique Downey			
Gender: F	**Age:** 57		**Marital Status:** Married
Education: RN, University of Louisville, MBA, Harvard			
Title: CEO			**Office Location:** Fort Worth
Reports To:	Board of Trustees		
Employment History:	Nurse for 7 years; medical sales for 5 years. Hired at Pharmiceaux at 36, district manager at 42, regional manager at 52, CEO at 56.		
Personality:	Caring, professional, very efficient and well-organized.		
Notes:	Works an 11-hour day; frequent public speaker.		
Grapevine:	Possible cabinet position with the Clinton Administration.		

<table>
<tr><td colspan="4">Name: Melanie Franmeister</td></tr>
<tr><td colspan="2">Gender: F</td><td>Age: 50</td><td>Marital Status: Married</td></tr>
<tr><td colspan="4">Education: BS, University of British Columbia; MBA, University of Cincinnati</td></tr>
<tr><td colspan="3">Title: VP, Sales</td><td>Office Location: Fort Worth</td></tr>
<tr><td>Reports To:</td><td colspan="3">CEO</td></tr>
<tr><td>Employment History:</td><td colspan="3">Peace Corps (2 years); 5 years as a Brand Assistant and Brand Manager at Procter and Gamble. Hired by Pharmiceaux as Marketing Planner, decided to enter sales force, went from sales manager to VP, sales.</td></tr>
<tr><td>Personality:</td><td colspan="3">Outgoing, caring, good sense of humor, goal-oriented.</td></tr>
<tr><td>Notes:</td><td colspan="3">Well-liked by subordinates; willing to take risks; open-door policy; into New Age music and crystals.</td></tr>
<tr><td>Grapevine:</td><td colspan="3">Being recruited by competition.</td></tr>
</table>